Screening
Social Justice

Screening
Social Justice

Brave New
Films and
Documentary
Activism

**Sherry B.
Ortner**

DUKE UNIVERSITY PRESS *Durham and London* 2023

© 2023 DUKE UNIVERSITY PRESS

All rights reserved

Printed in the United States of America on acid-free paper ∞

Designed by Matthew Tauch

Typeset in Arno Pro, Helvetica LT Std Ultra Compressed, and Alegreya Sans by Westchester Publishing Services

Library of Congress Cataloging-in-Publication Data

Names: Ortner, Sherry B., [date] author.

Title: Screening social justice : Brave New Films and documentary activism / Sherry B. Ortner.

Description: Durham : Duke University Press, 2023. | Includes bibliographical references and index.

Identifiers: LCCN 2022030441 (print)

LCCN 2022030442 (ebook)

ISBN 9781478016861 (hardcover)

ISBN 9781478019510 (paperback)

ISBN 9781478024132 (ebook)

Subjects: LCSH: Brave New Films. | Documentary films—Production and direction—Political aspects. | Documentary films—Political aspects. | Alternative mass media—Political aspects. | BISAC: PERFORMING ARTS / Film / Genres / Documentary | SOCIAL SCIENCE / Activism & Social Justice

Classification: LCC PN1995.9.D6 O897 2023 (print) | LCC PN1995.9.D6 (ebook) | DDC 070.1/8—dc23/eng/20221003

LC record available at https://lccn.loc.gov/2022030441

LC ebook record available at https://lccn.loc.gov/2022030442

Cover art: Hand and camera illustration by Shepard Fairey. Detail from the Brave New Films company logo. Courtesy of the artist and Obey Giant Art.

To Tim and Gwen
With love as always
***

In memory of my dear cousin
Richard Ortner

Pessimism of the intellect, optimism of the will.

REVOLUTIONARY ACTIVIST ANTONIO GRAMSCI

Life's a bitch. You've got to go out and kick ass.

POET MAYA ANGELOU

Contents

Preface

This study is based on ten months of fieldwork at an independent film production company called Brave New Films, which makes critical films designed to get people politically activated. I conducted fieldwork at the company's office/production site, and at live screenings of their films, between May 2019 and March 2020. As they were making a film about voter suppression during my fieldwork, with implications for (among many other things) the upcoming presidential election, I planned to continue the fieldwork through the election in November 2020. But the COVID-19 pandemic lockdown went into effect in March, the work of the company was disrupted as people shifted to working at home, and I was unable to continue the fieldwork at the office. At the same time, and for the same reasons, live screenings were suspended, so that part of the work was truncated as well. And, like everyone else, I had no idea when all this would return to "normal." So I decided to write this short book based on my existing data.

The writing of the first draft took place between March 2020 and February 2021, a period that covered the final year of the increasingly out-of-control Trump presidency; the ongoing, and also apparently out-of-control, COVID pandemic; and the shocking events following the election, including the violent storming of the Capitol by right-wing extremists on January 6, 2021. The work on the book revisions took place between February and September 2021. Trump was out of office, but the far right continued to threaten in many arenas. Among other things they militantly resisted vaccinations, masking, and indeed any and all rational public health measures, thus prolonging the pandemic. People continued to get very sick, and to die, in large numbers, but even for those who managed to stay healthy, life at every level—home, work, school, friendship, kinship—continued to be massively disrupted. Meanwhile enormous fires raged out of control in my home state of California, and extreme weather conditions battered other parts of the country.

It all has felt, and continues to feel, like we are looking at the front edge of the apocalypse, and I have allowed some comments on this to intrude into the text. Beyond the comments, the whole mood of the text is colored by these events, and it has been an effort to continue to believe that we can save the present world, no less make a better one. Thus I have to remind myself at every turn of the epigraphs for this book, Antonio Gramsci's maxim "Pessimism of the intellect, optimism of the will," and Maya Angelou's pithy comment "Life's a bitch. You've got to go out and kick ass."

Acknowledgments

I am incredibly grateful to all those who facilitated this project. For valuable background conversations and/or emails in the early stages, I thank Johanna Blakley, Violaine Roussel, William Roy, and Edward Walker.

Huge thanks to Barbara Boyle, who made the initial contact with Robert Greenwald for me and got me in the door.

Deepest thanks to Robert Greenwald, who not only let me in the door at Brave New Films but also gave me several key interviews, included me in several meetings, and allowed me to eavesdrop on conversations during production. He also informed the staff that I had his support for the project, which opened the rest of the doors at the company.

Thanks to Jill Ettinger for very kindly coordinating my schedule of meetings with staff people, and thanks to all those staffers for their thoughtful interviews: Laurie Ashbourne, Casey Cooper Johnson, Danielle Cralle, Jill Ettinger, Justin Harrison, Kimber Kissel, Justin Mickens, Jim Miller, Anne Phillips, Chris Rogers, Omar Samad, Tahil Sharma, and Devin Smith. Special thanks to Anne Phillips, Laurie Ashbourne, and Jim Miller, who kindly made themselves available for follow-up interviews.

Many thanks to the fellows and interns who gamely submitted to individual and/or group interviews: Francisco Aviles Pino Jr., Serena Francisco, Tatyana Garnett, Maya Hernandez, Noely Mendoza, Naomi Miyamoto, and Josué Muñoz.

Many, indeed most, of the people I interviewed at Brave New Films, whether regular staff, fellows, or interns, have in one way or another moved on or up. I still think about them all, wonder what they're doing, and hope things are going well for them.

And so we move on to the writing of this book, and all the help and support from friends and colleagues that went into it.

For early feedback, I thank my terrific colleagues in Culture/ Power/Social Change (CPSC), our interest group in the Department of Anthropology at UCLA. I presented a very early and still very fuzzy version of the introduction and received—as always—super-sharp comments from the group. I scribbled down a few names at the time—Hannah Appel, Lieba Faire, Akhil Gupta, Gail Kligman, Peter Kurie, Purnima Mankekar, and Alex Thomson—but I know there were others as well, and I'm sorry about those names that are missing. A big collective thanks to the group that has been my intellectual lifeline since I came to UCLA.

For all their extremely smart, honest, and insightful feedback on the full manuscript, I thank my friends and colleagues Philippe Bourgois, John Caldwell, Robert Greenwald, Laurie Kain Hart, Gail Kligman, Peter Kurie, Abigail Stewart, and Timothy Taylor, and two very knowledgeable anonymous readers for Duke University Press. I am, as always, especially grateful to Tim Taylor, as he was both my first and last reader, and made a huge difference at both ends.

For editorial savvy and insight, as well as just the right balance between enthusiasm, criticism, and support, I thank Ken Wissoker of Duke University Press.

For technical support, I thank Maya Gutierrez, who did an excellent job of transcribing interviews and film transcripts.

And finally, thanks yet again to Tim Taylor, for sharing with me *la belle vie* of good food, wine, conversation, movies, gardens, friends, and love.

Introduction

There is a very long history of connection between "powerful texts" and radical social movements. By "powerful texts" I mean texts, whether print or visual, that not only circulate widely but also have the capacity to inspire us to imagine better worlds and to draw together social groups, communities, and networks of people to try to bring about change. They have this capacity because they claim to represent "truth" in some form, and because their truthfulness is widely accepted.

Studies of the role of the Bible in the English Revolution of the seventeenth century (Hill 1972), or the role of newspapers in the American and French Revolutions of the eighteenth (B. Anderson 1983; Habermas [1962] 1991; Eley 1992), emphasize the ways these texts were read and discussed in collective contexts, whether religious congregations or urban coffeehouses, and opened up vistas of alternative ways of organizing social life and political authority. The Bible and newspapers may appear to be very different things, claiming very different kinds of "truth." But they had in common the capacity to engage people at both the level of intense social intercourse and the level of powerful ideas and meanings. As a result, people came to see themselves as parts of new collectivities, to feel that the world could be changed for the better, and—under the right circumstances—to act on those feelings.

Closer to the present, and closer to the subject of this book, we may consider Liberation Theology and the development of "Base Ecclesial Communities" (BECs) in Latin America. The analogy is very close to the English example (see Hill 1993), involving the reading and (re)interpretation of the

Bible in small local groups and congregations, with an explicit commitment to favoring the poor and challenging the structures of power (Gutiérrez 1973). Drawing parallels between their own lives and biblical stories, and rereading the Bible in terms of its more radical implications, people in these groups came to see themselves as politically empowered actors. In the Brazilian case, for example, the BECs played an important role during the period of extreme military repression in the 1960s and '70s. Among other things, they "offered a proven consciousness-raising methodology and a participatory form of education to train local informed citizens, many of whom later became grassroots activists" (Vásquez 1998, 52).

The arguments in all of these cases are, needless to say, vastly more complex, but the general point is that what I am calling powerful texts have historically played a significant role in the formation of radical and even revolutionary politics. Accepted as capturing some important form of truth (transcendental truth in the case of the Bible; objective and pragmatically useful truth in the case of newspapers), they have served as inspirations and catalysts for the formation of intensely engaged social groups and networks. People not only read them; they talked about them, argued about them, and sometimes used them as a basis of radical action.

The present book is an ethnographic study of Brave New Films (BNF), a nonprofit company that makes documentaries intended to inspire and provoke progressive political activism. They use their films as would-be "powerful texts" that embody a certain form of truth-telling, and that ideally serve as inspiration and organizing tools for the pursuit of social justice. Brave New Films also relies heavily on a system of in-person screenings, in which people can discuss and debate the issues of the films and can ideally develop courses of action to bring about progressive social change. Although the historical and cultural contexts are very different, and although we are looking at film rather than print media, it is not much of a stretch to say that BNF seeks to put in motion the same kind of dynamic just sketched for those earlier social movements.

I will look at Brave New Films partly through their films, and partly through their on-the-ground production, distribution, and organizing activities. I situate the company within the spectrum of alternative and radical media, especially but not exclusively within the terrain of documentary film, which has a long history of activist filmmaking. The overall argument of the book is framed in terms of the production of what media scholars Paula Rabinowitz (1994) and Angela Aguayo (2019) have called "political agency." I will explain this idea more fully below, and throughout the book, but the central point is to ask how different aspects of Brave New Films' work seek to shape and develop people's capacity and inclination to act in the public sphere on behalf of issues of social justice.

I begin from the assumption, associated particularly with the work of Paulo Freire ([1970] 2000, 2004), that people on the outside or underside of power are unlikely to do this spontaneously. The reasons vary by social location: the impoverished peasants and urban slum dwellers whom Freire worked with saw themselves weak and powerless; more privileged groups may think that many problematic social issues do not apply to them; and both groups are likely to think the system is very hard to change anyway. Thus a sense of political agency, including the idea that the system is in fact changeable, must be cultivated, and this cultivation process is the lens through which I will view the work of Brave New Films.

I will elaborate more on these themes below, but before I get to that I must confront the relationship between this book and real-world events during its making.

Engaged Anthropology and the Real World

We live in frightening times. The research for this book was conducted mostly in 2019, during the penultimate year of the presidency of Donald Trump, whom it is hard not to see as at least a protofascist. Among other things, throughout his presidency he had been actively seeking to subvert the democratic process and the rule of law and to encourage the rise of white supremacist and other movements of hatred and violence. The drafting of this book was mostly done in 2020, when Trump was increasingly unhinged and the COVID-19 pandemic was raging, in large part because of Trump's (non)decisions and (in)actions.

More frightening still is the realization that Trump as an individual is only the tip of an iceberg. Right-wing extremism has been growing at both the top of the class structure—among individual billionaires and among the leaders of the Republican Party—and throughout the rest of the system—in the form of (among other things) unruly gangs of white thugs, showing up at demonstrations armed and in battle gear, and displaying hateful insignia like swastikas and Confederate flags. One public joining of those two social levels was the right-wing storming of the US Capitol in January 2021, which was egged on by Trump and a significant number of Republican legislators and left several people dead.

In this same period, however, we have also seen the emergence of extraordinary mass resistance movements, including—to name just a few prominent examples—#BlackLivesMatter and all the other groups fighting against white supremacy and racial violence; Occupy Wall Street and all the other groups fighting against economic injustice and inequality; and an updated/upgraded feminist movement, starting with the massive Women's March in January 2017, and including its most recent avatar, #MeToo, fighting against patriarchal violence and gender inequality.

In relation to all of this and to ongoing violent racist policing, anthropology as a discipline has increasingly taken the "engaged turn" (Hale 2008; Low and Merry 2010; Abu-Lughod 2019; Ortner 2019), the attempt to integrate scholarship and a commitment to social justice. This involves both the critical study of the workings of power, inequality, and violence—what I elsewhere called "dark anthropology" (Ortner 2016)— and the study of various forms of opposition to power, from "everyday forms of resistance" (Scott 1985) to organized social movements (Juris 2008; Graeber 2009; Appel 2014; Shah 2019; and see chapter 3). Engaged anthropologists have challenged the idea that rigorous scholarship and a commitment to social justice are mutually exclusive, and they are increasingly using their scholarly work to not only describe the world but also critique it and perhaps help to change it for the better.

I have done work on both sides, as it were, of the engaged turn. With respect to issues of power and domination, I have done extensive work on patriarchal power, most recently as it intersects with capitalism (2014) and racism (2020). With respect to oppositional activism, I have written on "resistance" from a theoretical point of view (1995, 2006), as well as documenting Sherpa strikes and other forms of resistance throughout the history of Himalayan mountaineering (1999). Most recently, in counterpoint to the discussion of "dark anthropology," I looked briefly at some of the newer work by anthropologists on social movements, which I will discuss more fully in chapter 3.[1]

In the present work I look at oppositional politics from another angle, namely, from the point of view of an organization that is dedicated to *generating* political activism, to making it happen. As any political organizer knows, mobilizing people to act against power is no easy thing; it requires a good deal of creativity and multiple strategies. Brave New Films tries to do this with documentary film, and the point of this book is to understand how they (try to) do it.

My approach throughout is thus classically ethnographic, in the sense of trying to understand BNF's work from their internal point of view, rather than from some external critical perspective. While one could certainly develop a variety of critiques—of the company founder and president, Robert Greenwald; of the films; of the whole BNF operation—that would be part of a different kind of project. The present book extends my interest in forms of resistance in general, and the use of film and media for this purpose in particular.

Film and Social Activism: A Brief History

There is an ongoing debate, dating at least to the Cold War in the 1950s, over whether it is a good idea for filmmakers to incorporate their own political perspectives in their films. On the whole, the culture of filmmaking in the United States, even including a significant segment of alternative or independent filmmaking, has leaned strongly against it. The idea is that the American public does not like to be told what to think. The ideal film, in this view, presents the audience with a range of information and positions and allows viewers to come to their own conclusions. Anything that is "too political," that is slanted too far in one direction, will be described as having too much "message" or "agenda" and risks being labeled "propaganda" (Ortner 2013a). This view is institutionalized in an endlessly inventive range of wisecracks: Movie mogul Samuel Goldwyn famously said, "If I wanted to send a message, I'd call Western Union."[2] Questioned about the political implications of his film *The Three Burials of Melquiades Estrada* (2005), Tommy Lee Jones said, "If I wanted to make a political statement, I'd run for Congress."[3] Film scholar Bill Nichols said about political documentary in general, "If you want to influence legislation, hire a lobbyist" (2016a, 225).[4] Filmmaker Michael Moore said, "If I wanted to hear a sermon, I'd go to church" (in Nick Fraser 2019, 222). And so on.

I mention all this as contrastive background to the fact that Brave New Films is, by almost any measure, "very political." Further, by "political" in this book I will always mean politics that are basically "on the left" unless otherwise specified. There is also a smaller but not insignificant body of right-wing documentary filmmaking—both historically, as in Leni Riefenstahl's *Triumph of the Will* (1935), and currently, as in Dinesh D'Souza's *Obama's America* (2016). But right-wing film and media are beyond the scope of the present book, except insofar as they are targets of Brave New Films' critiques.

There are certain limits on the degree to which, and the ways in which, Brave New Films can be "very political." In particular, because of their nonprofit status (more on that in a moment), they cannot endorse any candidate in the sphere of electoral politics. Other than that, they manage to find ways to express strong political opinions and commitments without violating that status. For example, as Jim Miller, who was executive director at the time of the research, explained, there are different accounts in the budget with different tax statuses, C3 and C4. He clarified further: "C3 is tax deductible, C4 is not tax deductible. On the C4, you can be more overtly political. You can do more overt advocacy. You still can't say, vote for or against somebody, but the line is different. The line is kind of gray, so every piece of work that we do, we run by the lawyers, to make sure that we are doing it correctly" (interview, June 24, 2019). In other words, by working the options, Brave New Films is able to mount strong and explicit critiques of virtually any aspect of injustice when and how they see fit.

In doing this work, they join a long lineage of "committed filmmaking" (Waugh 1984) that began in the 1920s and is represented almost entirely by documentaries. This is both an exciting story in itself and a necessary backdrop to understanding where they are coming from. I thus offer here a very brief history of activist filmmaking over the course of the twentieth century, drawing primarily on work in cinema and media studies. Most of the sources for this part of the history were compiled in the 1980s and '90s, responding to a surge in documentary filmmaking in the 1960s and '70s (Rosenthal 1980; Waugh 1984; Steven 1985; Rabinowitz 1994; Winston 1995).

The story starts in the 1920s, with filmmakers Dziga Vertov and Sergei Eisenstein in the Soviet Union, and Joris Ivens in Europe, all of whom were inspired by early communist dreams of the future. Ivens in particular made films intentionally meant to activate audiences: "After informing and moving audiences, [a film] should agitate—mobilize them to be active in connection with the problems shown in the film" (quoted in Nick Fraser 2019, 96). Ivens's most famous film, *The Spanish Earth* (1937), about the Spanish Civil War, is said to have "raised enough funds to send eighteen ambulances to the Spanish front" (Waugh 1984, xxii). In the United Kingdom, John Grierson launched what came to be called a Griersonian "school" of filmmaking, focusing, among other things, on the physical labor of men within the disappearing traditional occupations and growing industrialization of capitalism.[5] On the American side, filmmakers of that era were "document[ing] as forcibly as possible the social struggles of the thirties: foreclosures, evictions, strikes" (e.g., *Native Land* [Hurwitz and Strand, 1937–41]; see Rosenthal 1980, 9–10).

The radical filmmaking of the 1920s and '30s was cut off by World War II, as both Hollywood and the documentarians were recruited to make films supporting the war effort and the nation (Combs and Combs 1994). It was further cut off by the rise of Senator Joseph McCarthy and his witch hunt for communists, both real and imagined. Its resurgence begins in the late 1960s, with (among other things) the founding of the filmmaking collective Newsreel, which made films specifically "to organize and mobilize working class and Third World peoples," to serve as "direct organizing tools" (Nichols 1978, 10; [1972] 2016; Renov 2004).

The 1960s and '70s saw an enormous growth and diversification in documentary filmmaking, a good part of it "political" in the sense discussed here. Radical filmmaking flourished in Latin America, Africa, and other parts of the global South, contributing both important films and new theoretical perspectives. These converged in what Argentinian filmmakers Fernando Solanas and Octavio Getino called "a Third Cinema" (1976), described as "independent in production, militant in politics, and experimental in language" (Shohat and Stam 1994, 261). Solanas and Getino made one of the major films to come out of that era, *The Hour of the Furnaces* (1968), about neocolonialism and resistance in Argentina. Others included *Memories of Underdevelopment* (Gutiérrez Alea 1968) from Cuba, *The Battle of Chile* (Guzmán 1975) from Chile, and in Africa, the work of Ousmane Sembène of Senegal (e.g., the feature film *Xala* [1974], discussed in Gabriel 1985).

In the United States, too, filmmakers were responding to the political turbulence of the times: the Black urban uprisings of the 1960s, the

Vietnam War, the emergence of the New Left and the women's movement, and more. At one level there is a continuity of subject matter; the primary target is generally the state, whether the colonial state in the European context (e.g., Gillo Pontecorvo's *The Battle of Algiers*, 1966), or the imperial state (e.g., Emile de Antonio's *In the Year of the Pig*, 1968) in the American context.[6] There is also a continuity with films about working-class/labor issues (e.g., Barbara Kopple's *Harlan County, U.S.A.*, 1976). At the same time there is a blurring—thanks to the women's movement—between the personal and the political, and we see the strong emergence of documentary that seeks to show what goes on behind closed doors, whether institutional (e.g., Frederick Wiseman's *Titicut Follies*, 1967) or familial (e.g., Craig Gilbert's *An American Family*, 1973).

The 1980s and '90s saw the beginnings of the independent film movement, including both narrative and documentary film. It was during those decades that the effects of neoliberal economic policies and corporate globalization were beginning to make themselves felt. Plants were closing, jobs were drying up, and the economy began a process of polarization in which the 1 percent got richer, the poor got poorer, and the middle class began to disintegrate. In this context, along with the proliferation of high-quality work on race (e.g., Spike Lee's *Four Little Girls*, 1997) and gender/sexuality (e.g., Jennie Livingston's *Paris Is Burning*, 1990), we see the beginnings of the current stage of political documentary filmmaking, with a stronger focus on the dynamics of macro power—capitalism, corporatism, militarism, political subversion, and so forth. Key films in that genre in that late twentieth-century period included Michael Moore's *Roger and Me* (1989), in which Moore revisits his hometown of Flint, Michigan, where the closing of a General Motors plant had thrown thousands of people out of work; Barbara Trent's *Panama Deception* (1992), which exposes the real material and political reasons behind George H. W. Bush's invasion of Panama; and Mark Achbar and Peter Wintonick's *Manufacturing Consent: Noam Chomsky and the Media* (1993), which explores issues of bias and ideology in the press.

More recent work on activist documentary will appear in later chapters, including work by scholars in the ongoing "Visible Evidence" series on documentary film (starting with Gaines and Renov 1999), and a new wave of studies incorporating the impact of the internet on documentary activism (Marcus 2016; Aguayo 2019; Borum Chattoo 2020; Fallon 2019).

For now, I continue the overview of documentary history into the twenty-first century, with an emphasis on the conditions surrounding the founding of Brave New Films.

The Golden Age of Documentary

The period since the turn of the twenty-first century has been called "the golden age of documentary" (Kellner 2010, 30; McEnteer 2006, xiv). For one thing, it appears that more documentaries have been made in these decades than ever before. Although this is difficult to quantify, documentary scholar Caty Borum Chattoo provides some fairly telling numbers for at least the early part of this period: "Between 1996 and 2002, about 15 documentaries were released in US theaters each year, a number that tripled in 2003, reaching 50 [per year] in 2004" (2020, 49). In addition, documentaries began to receive much greater popular reception, as measured by both box office takes and awards. James McEnteer notes that "eight of the 10 top-grossing documentaries of all time were released" in the first decade of the twenty-first century, and most of those were "political" in one sense or another (2006, xii). These included Michael Moore's *Bowling for Columbine* (2002), about gun violence, which also won an Academy Award, and Davis Guggenheim's *An Inconvenient Truth* (2006), about global warming, which won an Academy Award and also garnered a Nobel Peace Prize for its star, Al Gore. The top film in this group was Michael Moore's *Fahrenheit 9/11* (2004), about Bush's invasion of Iraq, which won the Palme d'Or at the Cannes Film Festival—that is, the top prize in all categories, not simply among documentaries. *Fahrenheit 9/11* earned $120 million in domestic gross, still a record for a documentary film.

It is relevant to note here that documentary film has always been the least popular form of cinema. It has always garnered very small audiences, as many people find it boring and didactic, or partisan and propagandistic. Many (non)viewers are not simply uninterested but actively turned off by the genre. The explosion of documentary production and reception in this period is thus all the more remarkable.

There is general agreement that the conditions that fostered this development were related not only to the immediate political situation but also to the longer-term deterioration of the mediascape in the United States—

the shrinkage of the print media, the rise of Fox News and other right-wing media, and the overall entertainment-ization of television news.[7] As film scholar Douglas Kellner put it, "The Golden Age of Documentary was fueled in part by the bankruptcy of corporate news and information in the United States, in which a small number of corporations controlled the major television networks, as well as important newspapers and Internet sites" (Kellner 2010, 53). As documentary filmmaker Morgan Spurlock said, "The news we get from the TV, magazines, and newspapers is all watered down. Especially TV. . . . They're pulling a curtain down in front of our eyes and we're starved for information" (quoted in Mackey-Kallis 2008, 160).

The sheer absence of reliable information is part of the problem; another is the lack of a critical perspective on what is going on. Kellner's point is not simply that the media are not telling us enough, but also that they fail to take a critical, or even skeptical, perspective, and that they accept the official stories handed out by the administration or others in powerful positions. Writing about the Bush-Cheney era (2000–2008), he says, "The magnitude of social problems generated by the Bush-Cheney administration propelled documentary filmmakers to fill the gap provided by the conformity and complicity of corporate news media" (2010, 53). Or, as media scholar James McEnteer put it, "As mass media fail—now more than ever—to fulfill their watchdog role over public officials and policies, the importance of documentaries committed to telling the truth increases" (2006, 61).

At the same time, documentary film itself was evolving. As just sketched, it has a long history of committed/critical/activist filmmaking. Yet that was only one piece of the documentary spectrum, which included the traditional ethnographic film, as well as a kind of glossy/descriptive perspective on a wide range of other "general-interest" subjects (e.g., nature, travel). The explicitly critical/political film was in a minority, especially after World War II and during the McCarthy era, when such work was labeled unpatriotic. The majority position (with exceptions, of course) was neutrality: to avoid taking explicit, partisan positions on whatever the subject might be.

But this began to break down in the 1960s and '70s, in relation to the Vietnam War and the emergence of identity-based politics—the women's movement, the Black Power movement, and the gay rights movement. As has been widely noted and discussed, American culture and politics have become increasingly polarized around those issues, and this polarization soon made itself felt in electoral politics and the mediascape. The ultra-conservative Fox News soon emerged in this context. But an increasing number of documentary filmmakers also began to come out of the closet, as it were, and to take explicitly critical partisan positions on many issues. As one documentary filmmaker said, "The pose in the documentary world used to be, we're filmmakers and we're not out to change the political landscape. But Michael Moore unmasked us. We *are* out to change the political landscape" (Michael Paradies Shoob, quoted in Mackey-Kallis 2008, 159). And thus, as Douglas Kellner put it, "documentary filmmakers became the muckrakers of the time, exposing multiple injustices and social problems and speaking truth to power" (2010, 59).[8]

All of this began to come to a head beginning in the year 2000. In the closing decades of the twentieth century there was a great deal of anxiety about the millennial instant, that actual point of turnover from the twentieth to the twenty-first century. There were wild theories about how, at midnight, clocks and elevators would stop, computers would crash, planes would fall from the sky, and so forth. None of this came true, of course, and the whole idea of the turn of the millennium as an apocalyptic moment quickly faded away. Yet perhaps an argument can be made that the year 2000 was in fact an apocalyptic year in a different and less mystical sense, as the launching point of a disastrous sequence of political events: the controversial (to say the least) presidential election of 2000, the attack on the World Trade Center in 2001, and George W. Bush's decision to invade Iraq in 2003. With respect to Iraq, in turn, the invasion, the occupation, and the continuing military conflict became, for several observers, the twenty-first-century version of the Vietnam War (McEnteer 2006, xvii; Gaines 2015, 415).

Like the Vietnam War, the Iraq War triggered massive on-the-ground protest, including worldwide demonstrations in 2003. It is estimated that there were almost three thousand protests across the globe, with a total turnout of 36 million people.[9] Specifically with respect to the case at hand, the invasion triggered an enormous response among artists in general (Roussel and Lechaux 2010) and filmmakers in particular. In *Cinema Wars* (2010), Douglas Kellner devotes an entire chapter to films about the Iraq War, including more than thirty documentaries and another nine pages on Hollywood fiction films. Not all of the documentaries are antiwar.

Some are right-wing propaganda films meant to justify the war, and some take the point of view of the American soldiers on the ground and thus maintain neutrality. Yet others take the point of view of the Iraqis, who in the early stages of the war tended to be ambivalent about the Americans, although as things progressed they became increasingly critical and angry. But within this mix a few extremely critical films came out not simply against the war and its terrible violence and destruction, but also against the Bush administration and the defense contractors like Halliburton that made and sustained it, which brings us back to Brave New Films.

Brave New Films

Robert Greenwald was an active player in the growing political movement(s) of that time. Born and raised in New York, the son of professional parents, Greenwald had had a successful career in film and TV and had many contacts in the entertainment industry. During the run-up to the Iraq War, he and actor Mike Farrell formed a group called Artists United against the War, which acted as a kind of booking agency for anti-war celebrities to speak out against the war on high-visibility TV shows (Roussel and Lechaux 2010). He also made a life-changing decision to quit commercial entertainment and to commit fully to making critical political documentaries. The first of these that he directed was *Uncovered: The Whole Truth about the Iraq War* (2004), about how George W. Bush and company fabricated the "evidence" that Iraq had weapons of mass destruction, then coerced members of his administration, as well as much of the media, into endorsing his claims.[10] Greenwald made a second movie about the Iraq War two years later, *Iraq: The War Profiteers* (2006), about the outsourcing of many of the military functions to private contractors, who sacrificed the well-being of both the troops and their own employees for the bottom line of financial gain.

It was during this period that Greenwald began developing the company that became Brave New Films. Greenwald's vision for the company was innovative at many levels, including both production and distribution. On the production side, one of the main innovations was speed, as he was committed to making films that were closely responsive to ongoing current events. In his first five years of this work, he executive-produced two full-length films (*Unprecedented* [2002] and *Unconstitutional* [2004]) and directed four more (*Uncovered* [2004], *Outfoxed* [2004], *Wal-Mart* [2005], and *Iraq for Sale* [2006]), which is a remarkable record. As he put it: "Remember, back then, people weren't making politically timely documentaries: ours was really one of the first where we said, 'We're not going to do a documentary 10 years from today, we're doing it *now*, we want it out *now* and we want to affect the political dialog *now*'" (quoted in Haynes and Littler 2007, 26–27).

I want to emphasize the importance of this passion for timeliness. Much of the writing about Brave New Films, both journalistic and academic, emphasizes the originality and uniqueness of the company's distribution model, and I will get to that in a moment. But I think this sense of urgency, of needing to jump into the fray and start *doing something now*, is also a central part of the company's culture and identity. It accounts for the speed with which Greenwald embraced the internet and was willing to adjust his filmmaking practices to its strictures. And it accounts for the company's determination to document even the smallest of victories in relation to the subject of any particular film as evidence that they are making a difference *now*. While Brave New Films does offer a broad, long-term "vision statement" (which can be found in their annual reports)—"Our vision is an open democratic society that encourages rigorous debate, opportunity, and justice for all"—much of their energy goes into films and related media campaigns that, as we will see, are also emphatically designed to produce concrete outcomes in the present.

The next question was how to get large numbers of people to see the films, and the company undertook a series of experiments in distribution. These began with *Unprecedented: The 2000 Presidential Election* (2002), which was directed by some of Greenwald's friends. He said he and his friends "literally sold DVDs at a table outside the screenings" and would sometimes make a few hundred dollars, which seemed like a lot at the time: "I was beside myself. I was like, 'This is amazing.'" Next he directed the first of the Iraq War films, in partnership with the activist internet organization MoveOn.org. At first they were selling DVDs to the MoveOn membership and others, but then Eli Pariser, the wunderkind executive director of MoveOn at the time, suggested that they hold screenings at house parties, which they began to do with great success. Then a staff member, Jim Gilliam, approached Greenwald and said, "There's this new thing called YouTube, where you can post clips of your movies for free," and they tried that. "Two days later," Greenwald went on, Gilliam "walks in and shows me on his computer, 7,320 views." And Greenwald said, "Holy shit, if that were a theater it would be jammed!" And finally he took the quite radical step of deciding to make all of their films available for free: "I wanted to go more radical because I felt that our job was to reach people." Gesturing to the low popularity of documentary film, he said that charging money "limits your audience. Who is going to pay you to go to a documentary on a difficult subject?" (interview, May 15, 2019).

Greenwald had started the company as a conventional filmmaking enterprise, involving the standard strategies of searching for investors and a distributor, but was becoming fed up with scrounging for commercial backing, and more and more excited about the new distribution strategies. *Wal-Mart* was the turning point: "*Wal-Mart* was the full-tilt model: with *Wal-Mart* we planned the strategy a year in advance; we hired an organizer before I'd shot one frame of film; and even when we got offers to distribute it commercially, we turned them down, because by now we were firmly committed to this alternative method of distribution which had such a great effect" (quoted in Haynes and Littler 2007, 27).[11] This, then, is the model for Brave New Films today, and it is unique. All of their films are available for free on the internet, and they make virtually nothing from the films themselves. They operate like any nonprofit, raising money from grants and donations. At the same time, they devote at least half of their operations to generating screenings, partly through individuals and groups signing up via the BNF website, and partly by partnering with other nonprofits that in turn make the films available for screenings through their own networks.[12]

Political Agency

The main point of this book is, as noted earlier, to understand the ways in which the work of Brave New Films can be seen as cultivating "political agency" through its films and outreach. "Agency" refers to the human capacity to take intentional action in the world, both within and against (but never outside of) the constraints of society, culture, and history. It is a highly contested concept within the social sciences, and I have discussed some of those debates elsewhere (Ortner 2006). One of the issues concerns whether arguing for the (political) value of agency may appear to endorse and even celebrate a (neo)liberal model of the individualistic, Western-style social actor, pursuing his or her own agendas relatively free of social constraints.[13] This is certainly one of its implications, and agency in this sense can be seen as a form of privilege associated with status and power.

But the meaning of the term changes when it is set in a context of collective political action, and this is how I will be using it in this book. I draw inspiration on this subject from the work of Paulo Freire ([1970] 2000, 2004) and his discussion of *conscientização*, commonly translated as "consciousness-raising." Freire defines *conscientização* as the process by which oppressed people may become not merely objects on whom history does its work, but "subjects of history" who seek to both understand and change the world (2004). The core of the process is small-group discussion, and the outcome involves not only increased personal understanding of one's oppressed or exploited situation, but also an awareness of being part of a larger class or collectivity with whom one shares a similar positionality. In other words, there is a process in which individuals develop what we would call "agency"—a disposition to act for change, a sense of empowerment to act for change—but it is a social process on behalf of a social goal.

Freire was writing about impoverished peasants and urban slum dwellers in Brazil in the late 1960s and early '70s. His own work was geared toward secular education, but his strategy of using small-group discussions for political consciousness-raising was picked up by the hugely influential religious/political movement called Liberation Theology in Latin America in that era (Vásquez 1998) and thus received widespread application and recognition. Within that same period as well, and apparently independently, the nascent feminist movement in the United States was developing the idea of "consciousness-raising groups" as a tool for political organizing and potential action. The radical feminist group Redstockings put out a manifesto espousing essentially the same principles as Freire's concept of *conscientização*: "Our chief task at present is to develop female class consciousness through sharing experience and publicly exposing the sexist foundation of all our institutions. Consciousness-raising is not 'therapy,' which implies that the male-female relationship is purely personal, but the only method by which we can ensure that our program for [collective] liberation is based on the concrete realities of our lives" (Redstockings 1969). Consciousness-raising groups, seen as "the backbone of the Women's Liberation Movement," sprang up all over the country (Chicago Women's Liberation Union 1971). I do not mean to suggest that the gender oppression of mostly middle-class, mostly white women in that era was equivalent to the class oppression of very poor and subjugated Brazilian peasants and slum dwellers. But both movements, as well as all the politically critical filmmaking just discussed, were part of an era of widespread radicalization ("the Sixties") that drew in many people who were in some sense ready for, and open to, the kind of political consciousness-raising just described.

A variant of the consciousness-raising process was the reading group, where a group of people seeking to develop their own political thinking devoted themselves to reading some relevant texts or bodies of literature. We saw this earlier, in the context of the discussion of "powerful texts," with respect to BECs (Base Ecclesial Communities) in Latin America, reading, debating, and rethinking the Bible in politically critical terms. The Black Panthers in Oakland, California, began reading Marxist literature in that era (*The Black Panthers: Vanguard of the Revolution* [film], 2015), and there were no fewer than three Marxist-Feminist anthropology reading groups in New York City when I was living and working there in the 1970s. Full disclosure: at that time I belonged to both a consciousness-raising group, composed of young women anthropologists, which we called the Ruth Benedict Collective, and the Marxist-Feminist III (Uptown) reading group.[14]

The outcome of the consciousness-raising process, in whatever form, is ideally the production of what I am here calling "political agency," which includes both a heightened awareness and understanding of oppressive political realities and a heightened inclination or disposition to act against them. The idea of political agency in this sense is already part of some theorizing about activist documentary film. For example, historian Paula Rabinowitz, in the introduction to her study of the history and politics of American documentary, virtually echoes Paolo Freire: "The subject produced and provoked by documentary . . . is a subject of (potential) agency, an actor in history" (1994, 8). And in her study of "documentary resistance" (the book's title), Angela Aguayo makes the production of political agency a central theme, tying it particularly to the formation of collective identities among marginalized and subordinated groups in the contemporary United States (2019).

This book uses the case of Brave New Films to extend our thinking on this complex and important subject. I begin with a brief chapter situating Brave New Films within the larger American mediascape, and particularly within the world of "alternative media," media that positions itself against the mainstream media and the official versions of reality that they promulgate. Following that, I address the political agency question from three different perspectives. Chapter 2 provides an overview of BNF's output of film and video with respect to the portrayals of American politics they provide. The emphasis in the chapter is on the films as vehicles of truthful representation of reality, and on the point that the films are meant to create clarity and understanding—what I call "critical agency." Chapter 3, titled "Networked Agency," focuses on how Brave New Films is part of a world of social justice organizations, and on how the films circulate both "horizontally," through that world, and "down" to the grass roots through screenings. Chapter 4 looks deeply at one film, *Suppressed*, that was being made and circulated during my research. The chapter, titled "Affective Agency," focuses on the way the film appeals to feelings of both compassion and anger, and the way it "comes alive" for audiences during screenings. Together the three chapters seek to open up for the reader the capacity of these films to contribute to the production of political agency.

Winding its way through the chapters in different ways is the importance of truth to the process of political awakening and mobilization. Truth is central to the documentary project, and at the beginning of chapter 2 I address some of the debates and trade-offs over truth-telling within the documentary world. This discussion in turn underpins the substantive work of all of the chapters. Chapter 2 continues with an overview of BNF films, their approaches to truthful filmmaking, and their efforts to uncover not just factual truths but the deeper truth of the systemic nature of capitalism, racism, and (proto)fascism in the twenty-first-century United States. In chapter 3, about Brave New Films in the world of social movements, I build on the point that the films circulate in different activist contexts as "powerful texts," powerful because they are understood and felt to be true. And in chapter 4, about how *Suppressed* touches and provokes audiences emotionally, we learn ethnographically that this works in part because audiences are responding to what they feel is the honesty and credibility, the truthfulness, of the people who speak in the film.

In chapter 5 I turn to the question of impact. Although all BNF films are meant to contribute to the formation of political agency in general, each one also has its own specific focus, the specific form of injustice it seeks to challenge. Thus we—and the filmmaker—must also ask whether and how a given film brought about some of the specific changes it sought to make. I will answer this question at multiple levels, from the most concrete (e.g., specific pieces of legislation) to the most abstract (e.g., the expansion of activist publics). In this context I also return to Brave New Films as part of "alternative media" and ask about their success in challenging the versions of reality put out by the mainstream media. I will end by proposing that, alongside all those things, one of the most important forms of impact generated by Brave New Films and all the other work of the documentary movement may be the remobilization and revalidation of the importance of truth-telling itself.

1 Brave New Films in the Mediascape

It is hard to overstate the power of media, and it is as important to understand this as it is to understand the "economy" and the "politics" of the world we live in. While this book is based on a study of a single organization, the organization is part of the enormous American "mediascape," a term coined by anthropologist Arjun Appadurai (1990) to encompass all the forms of "public culture" (Appadurai and Breckenridge 1988) that circulate locally, nationally, and globally.

The mediascape can be examined at multiple levels and from a variety of perspectives.[1] At one level it consists of a landscape of on-the-ground companies and organizations, in which various media forms (film, TV, newspapers, etc.) and content are produced. This is the terrain of the "anthropology of media" (Askew and Wilk 2002; Ginsburg, Abu-Lughod, and Larkin 2002) and of "production studies" (Caldwell 2008, 2013; Mayer, Banks, and Caldwell 2009), and first I need to say a few words about those areas of research.

Media anthropology grew out of a robust earlier tradition of "visual anthropology," concerned mostly with studies of ethnographic film and photography (Ginsburg 1999; Mahon 2000).[2] In large part thanks to the pioneering work of Faye Ginsburg on Indigenous media starting in the 1990s (e.g., 1993, 1997), as well as key studies of "media worlds" by anthropologists Lila Abu-Lughod in Egypt (1995) and Purnima Mankekar in India (1999) in that same period, there was an important shift in the focus of the visual anthropology field: film and photography shifted from being seen primarily as *technologies* of anthropological research to being seen, at least in part, as important *objects* of such research. They also became parts of a much wider array of media forms as objects of study, including television, radio, recording industries, the internet, and more.[3]

Media anthropology, like anthropology in general, is committed to an ethnographic approach to the study of media. Ethnographic fieldwork, as all ethnographers know, involves long-term, whole-self immersion in particular social worlds, and allows one to gain a kind of deep and textured understanding of those worlds available through no other forms of research. Anthropologists have conducted ethnographic studies of media in a wide range of national and global contexts, and I will look briefly at some of those below. But scholars in other fields have also in some cases used ethnographic methods, and I want to note here the recent work of media studies scholar (and documentary filmmaker) John Caldwell. Caldwell has developed an ethnographic approach to what he calls "production studies" that involves delving deeply and critically into the viewpoints of workers in the media industries and seeking to understand those industries from those points of view (2008, 2013; see also Mayer, Banks, and Caldwell 2009).

Along with the commitment to ethnographic methodology, the other major dimension of media anthropology research involves looking at media within their larger social, cultural, and political contexts. As opposed to stereotypical "film studies," for example, which is heavily focused on the interpretation of films as relatively self-contained texts, media anthropology always asks questions about the relationship between text and (social) context. Here overlapping considerably with the sociology of media, "(cinema and) media studies" (CMS), and "cultural studies," anthropologists of media situate specific media organizations (like Brave New Films) and forms (like documentary film) within what Ginsburg, Abu-Lughod, and Larkin (2002) called "media worlds," that is, larger worlds of production, circulation, and reception, and larger structures of power and inequality.

If at one level the world of media is an empirical world of companies and organizations that can be studied ethnographically, at another level it is a conceptual system based on categorical distinctions that structure the mediascape as a whole. The empirical and conceptual aspects of the mediascape are not two separate entities but, rather, two different ways of looking at the same terrain. In this context, then, we regard the mediascape as one instance of what Pierre Bourdieu has called a "field of cultural production," a space that is both metaphorical and real, in which the actual process of producing cultural goods unfolds. Bourdieu (1993) divides any field of cultural production into a field of "large-scale production" and a field of "restricted production." Artists working within the large-scale field produce the more commercial and mass-oriented work, while artists working in restricted fields produce work that is both posed against commercial values and targeted to more narrowly defined aesthetically and/or politically defined audiences.

Within the various fields of media studies, this can be translated into the language of an opposition between "mainstream media" and "alternative media," an opposition that runs through all the different media forms. With respect to film, for example, "mainstream" refers to Hollywood movies, while "alternative" refers to independent film. With respect to print media, "mainstream" refers to the major (corporate) newspapers, while "alternative" refers to independent newspapers and magazines. And so forth. The opposition is very important in terms of understanding both the power of (mainstream) media and its limits, limits created precisely by the challenges of alternative media. Indeed, the absence of robust alternative media, and thus of challenges to mainstream media, is a central feature of a totalitarian state. Brave New Films is very much part of this alternative sector of the mediascape, and I will also look at them from this point of view.

Production Sites and Forms

Any independent filmmaker who wants to make a film that will actually go out into the world and reach audiences beyond their friends and family needs to either create their own production company (as Greenwald did) or find a producer/production company that commits to helping them finance, make, and distribute their film.

Production companies come in all shapes and sizes, from a one-person entity (a movie star or a filmmaker who self-incorporates) to the giant studios of Hollywood. Gaining research access to the major studios is extremely difficult (see Ortner 2010), but some ethnographers have developed creative work-arounds, and we are seeing important new work in this area (Caldwell 2008; Martin 2017). Here, however, I will focus on independent production companies. Many of these, although organizationally free-standing and independent of the Hollywood studios, nonetheless produce Hollywood-oriented films. They put together projects that are geared to Hollywood sensibilities and that they hope to sell to one of the major studios. But others are "independent" not only organizationally but also in terms of political and/or aesthetic values, and it is here that we find both independent (un-Hollywood, anti-Hollywood) feature films and virtually all documentaries.

Independent production companies are mainly concentrated in Los Angeles and New York. Their mission is to work closely with independent filmmakers to help them turn their ideas into films and to get those films out in the world. One that I came to know fairly well in the course of an earlier study of independent film (Ortner 2012, 2013b) was Los Angeles–based Bona Fide Productions, a two-man operation consisting of Albert Berger and Ron Yerxa. Bona Fide mainly produces narrative/fictional films, including such indie successes as *Little Miss Sunshine* (2006) and *Little Children* (2006). Many of their films, like these, are about middle-class American families, but the films are far from bourgeois depictions of life in those families. Rather, they bring out their weirdness, and sometimes their cruelty, challenging the viewer's expectations about the ordinary, the everyday, the "normal" in day-to-day American society.

I also conducted a brief study of a production company called Participant (formerly Participant Media) (Ortner 2017). This is a much bigger operation, more like a small studio, with both a narrative division and a documentary division. A recent big film of theirs on the narrative side was *Judas and the Black Messiah* (2021); a major success on the documentary side was *An Inconvenient Truth* (2006). Participant films seem less independent-spirited in terms of challenging viewers' assumptions about what is real and true and "normal" in our ordinary lives, but—as the titles just noted indicate—they have more of a social/political agenda than companies like Bona Fide, explicitly seeking to create "social impact."

Bona Fide and Participant and most other production entities are for-profit companies. Participant, again like most other production companies, is also fairly conventional in its organization, with a hierarchy of employees and, at the top, a sole male chief executive with final authority. At the opposite end of the spectrum, however, we find the filmmaking collectives, all nonprofit, all organized in relatively egalitarian ways and making films that are, on the whole, somewhat more culturally or politically radical. One of the most legendary of these, documented largely through the research of Bill Nichols (e.g., [1972] 2016), was Newsreel, which no longer exists. One of their most famous films is *Columbia Revolt* (1968), about the protests at Columbia University that played a major role in the radical politics of the 1960s. Another well-known collective is Kartemquin Films, which is still going strong in Chicago (Blumenthal and Rohrer 1980; Aguayo 2019).[4] They are perhaps most famous for *Hoop Dreams* (1994) and more recently *Minding the Gap* (2019), films that could be described as critically ethnographic, often about young people struggling against the race and class constraints of their lives.

Ranging beyond film, there have been several collectives dedicated to offering alternatives to mainstream journalism, in terms of both unmasking official misrepresentations and providing information for, and coverage of, social movement actions. One was Paper Tiger Television, "a largely volunteer collective" that was part of the Gulf Crisis TV (GCTV) project mobilized against the first invasion of Iraq in 1991 (Marcus 2016, 192–96). GCTV in turn served as something of a model for the creation of the collectively run Independent Media Center (IMC), commonly known as Indymedia, which began as an operation for the collection and distribution of accurate information during the protests at the World Trade Organization's 1999 meeting in Seattle. Indymedia represent themselves as "a network of collectively run media outlets for the creation of radical, accurate, and passionate tellings of the truth. We work out of love and inspiration for people who continue to work for a better world, despite corporate media's distortions and unwillingness to cover the efforts to free humanity" (quoted in Stringer 2013, 322–23). Indymedia is beloved of most activists. In his ethnography of the Direct Action Network, for example, David Graeber wrote, "As a tool of practical de-alienation, and aid in self-organization, Indymedia transformed everything" (2009, 473).

Brave New Films is an odd mixture of the two types of production companies just discussed. It shares the radical spirit of the collectives and, like the collectives, is not-for-profit. Organizationally, however, it is more like many of the for-profit production companies, with a traditional hierarchical structure. I here offer a brief ethnographic sketch of the form, and some of the spirit, of the company as it was operating at the time of my research.

A Brief Workplace Ethnography

Brave New Films occupies a 1960s-era former motel in Culver City, California, across the street from the southern wall of the enormous Sony Pictures (formerly MGM) studio lot. There are about fourteen full-time employees, plus several short-term contract employees, one-year fellows, and one-semester interns.[5] Many share offices, in which almost everyone creates their own work bubble with headphones. All of them can fit inside Greenwald's office (one of the larger motel rooms), where he holds staff meetings once or twice a month.

The staff can be roughly divided into three groups—executive, production, and distribution/outreach. The executive group (though it doesn't have a formal name) consists of Robert Greenwald, the studio's president; an executive director, who is both chief of staff and main fundraiser; a development associate, who assists with the fundraising; a vice president of operations, who oversees the business affairs of the company; and a tech associate producer, who is in charge of, as he put it, "logistics at every phase of production," including managing the server, the studio space, and the company's equipment. The production group consists of a head of production; a number of coproducers, who actually put the films together (under Greenwald's direction); and a lead editor, who does most of the final film editing work.[6] The distribution/outreach group consists of a director of strategy and distribution, who serves as head of the combined social media and outreach operations; a social media manager, who orchestrates everything that goes out over social media; an outreach director, who lines up screenings of the films and establishes partnerships with social justice organizations; and a faith program manager, who specializes in outreach to faith communities for screenings and partnerships.

I'll have more to say about the outreach and distribution staff and their work in chapter 3, when I discuss BNF's links to wider social movements, and I'll have more to say about the producers and their work in chapter 4, when I discuss the making of one of the films. The main point for now is simply the distinctive structure of the company, with its equal commitment to production and (a particular kind of) distribution.

The lines of authority in this system are very clear. Greenwald is the director of record for all of the films; in addition, everything that goes into or out of that office goes through his hands. Aware of the history of documentary production collectives just sketched, I asked in my first interview with him how decisions were made in the company, and whether there was any kind of collective decision-making process. He said—with a smile—that while he is always willing to listen to suggestions and opinions from the staff, he does not believe in collective decision-making and makes all final decisions himself.

Greenwald is committed to diversity in hiring; the staff is fairly balanced in terms of gender and is also very racially and ethnically diverse. The diversity is recognized by all as a good thing, but it also occasionally produces some tensions. As the two most powerful members of the staff, Greenwald and (at the time) executive director Jim Miller, are white and male, differences of opinion between them and staff, and exercises of authority by them over staff, are always susceptible to being read in racial, ethnic, or gender terms. But these and other aspects of office social relations would be the subject of a different kind of study, and I will not be discussing them in this book. I will only note here that working at Brave New Films always entailed a lot of pressure on everyone—in terms of deadlines; in terms of Greenwald's high standards of performance; and in terms of the speed and intensity with which he wants to work. There was thus always a good deal of staff turnover, as well as reorganization of staff positions, no doubt based on all of the above factors. More than half of the people who were there at the time of my research are now gone.

To give the reader a tiny taste of the pressure of working at Brave New Films, I offer a note from the walking tour I was given at the beginning of the research. BNF operates as a kind of ministudio, with multiple production projects underway simultaneously, and at that time (May 2019), three different films were in progress in three different suites in the motel. In one suite, coproducer Omar Samad was working on a video for the series *Following Their Lead: Youth in Action*, about high school–aged activists and their projects. In another suite the next major project was already brewing: director of production Justin Harrison was working with an intern on developing a script for the next film. (This has now come out: *Racially Charged: America's Misdemeanor Problem* [2021].) Next, distributed over several suites, coproducer Casey Cooper Johnson, associate producer Laurie Ashbourne, lead editor Chris Rogers, and various fellows and interns, not to mention Greenwald himself, were working intensely on the current main project, a film about voter suppression called *Suppressed: The Fight to Vote*. At the end of my tour I was turned over to a somewhat harried-looking Laurie Ashbourne, who told me that they had just been given a hard September deadline for *Suppressed*, so it was "all hands on deck." Meanwhile, the social media people were trying to get a jump on the media campaign for *Suppressed*, pressuring the production people for access to some clips from the film, even though they weren't quite ready yet. And all that was in May, so things only got more intense from then on, as the September deadline approached.

Mainstream and Alternative Media

The question of the power of media in a broad sense was central to discussions of the onset and impact of "modernity," starting in the early twentieth century. One enormously influential line of discussion begins with Horkheimer and Adorno's critical study of the Hollywood "culture industry" ([1944] 2006), working with a Marxist-inspired theory of ideological domination, and arguing for the power of media to impose the worldview of dominant classes on "the masses." Under the influence of the later cultural studies movement (R. Williams 1977; Hall et al. 1980; Hall 1992; Grossberg, Nelson, and Treichler 1992), this work has grown increasingly sophisticated over time, particularly in terms of emphasizing how audiences actively engage with what they see and hear, and thus should not be assumed to be passive dupes of the media. This work has also become vastly more diverse, moving far beyond a homogeneous notion of "the masses" to incorporate perspectives from feminism (e.g., Traube 1992; Jones 2010; Press and Tripodi 2021), critical race theory (e.g., Lopez 2020), and post/colonial studies (e.g., Shohat and Stam 1994). Taken together, these bodies of work have set the terms of a framework that continues to play out in important ways in contemporary media studies (e.g., Lazere 1987; Ohmann 1996; Durham and Kellner 2006).

Using a different language, and focusing more on news media than film and entertainment, a related line of discussion begins from a division of the media world into "mainstream media" and "alternative media." This distinction, as I said earlier, is a conceptual opposition that runs through the entire mediascape—that is, every form of media will have its own "mainstream" and "alternative" types. Moreover, the opposition can appear *within* any given media type, such that, for example, "Hollywood" might produce independent-style films—more aesthetically and/or politically ambitious—along with their more "mainstream" blockbuster fare. For simplicity's sake, however, I will treat the two categories as if they referred to relatively fixed and separate entities in the world.

Mainstream media (like the "culture industry") are understood to be the voice of the dominant culture, and to be enormously powerful, imposing what might be called official versions of reality on the public in ways that make them seem natural, normal, sheer common sense. One of the best statements on this point comes from Todd Gitlin's study of the role of the media in the making and breaking of the New Left in the 1960s: "The media bring a manufactured public world into private space. From within their private crevices, people find themselves relying on the media for concepts, for images of their heroes, for guiding information, for emotional charges, for recognition of public values, for symbols in general, even for language. Of all the institutions of daily life, the media specialize in orchestrating everyday consciousness—by virtue of their pervasiveness, their accessibility, their centralized symbolic capacity. They name the world's parts, they certify reality *as* reality" (Gitlin 1980, 1–2). But again, this "reality" is never neutral; it is itself shaped by the worldview and interests of dominant classes and groups. Thus, although the mechanisms of persuasion vary between the different types of mainstream media, the general point is that they are all invested, one way or another, in supporting dominant cultural norms and existing social and political arrangements (see, e.g., Hall et al. 1980; Herman and Chomsky 1988). With respect to news coverage, for example, the mainstream press, radio, and TV networks are reliant on corporate funding, and they depend on continuing access to centers of power for their information. They thus rarely question the status quo. They do not necessarily lie, but they largely tell the official version of the truth, which, from the perspective of alternative media, is often itself full of lies, half-truths, and cover-ups.

At the same time, they effectively block attempts to tell the truth. Todd Gitlin's account of the omissions and distortions of mainstream media coverage of the New Left in the 1960s shows the ways in which, and the degree to which, the mainstream media stack the decks against the success of social movements that try to provide an account of reality that differs from the official narrative (1980). David Graeber tells a virtually identical story with respect to media coverage and noncoverage of major protest actions in the first decade of the 2000s. He writes, for example, of the near noncoverage of the massive protests at the inauguration of George W. Bush in 2001, which he describes as the "second largest inaugural protests in American history" (2009, 441). When pressed for an explanation, a *New York Times* representative replied that they regarded the protests as "staged events" and therefore "not news" (441).

Alternative media, on the other hand (see, e.g., Armstrong 1984; Downing 2001; Hamm 2008), provide both critiques of the mainstream media and theoretically more truthful accounts of the real world. The two are inextricably tied together. A large part of showing the truth about the world involves deconstructing and debunking the version of the world being put out by the mainstream media in the first place. We will see this clearly in the next chapter when I look at Brave New Films' political documentaries. One of the company's most famous films is *Outfoxed: Rupert Murdoch's War on Journalism* (2004), in which they take apart the right-wing representational strategies of Fox News. And while Fox News is quite far to the right of the "mainstream," even the so-called liberal media are seen, from this point of view, as part of a relatively conservative continuum that rarely challenges existing structures of money and power. Most BNF films involve the double move just noted, both challenging the mainstream version of events and trying to show the world "as it really is."

Alternative media tend to be somewhat more accessible for ethnographic research and are among the key areas of media anthropology attention. Anthropologists and ethnographically inclined scholars in other fields have been producing a growing body of closely textured studies of alternative media organizations both at home and abroad. There are ethnographic studies of public and independent television in the United States (Dornfeld 1998; Fish 2013); of independent film (including documentary) in the United States (Ortner 2013b); and of an independent journalism organization in the United States (Stringer 2013). There is also a growing body of studies of community media production in other parts of the world—Afghanistan (Edwards 2005), the Dominican Republic (Gregory 2007, chap. 3), Venezuela (Schiller 2018), Nigeria (Larkin 2008)—and of Indigenous media projects in Australia (Ginsburg 1993), Alaska (Ginsburg 2002), and the Amazon rain forest (Turner 2002). In all of these cases we see groups of citizens responding to misrepresentation or neglect by mainstream media by taking the means of media production into their own hands to show and tell the truth from their own point of view.

Alternative media have infinitely less money and power than mainstream media. Nonetheless, most observers agree that the messages of alternative media do work their way into the mainstream, if not exactly in the ways their purveyors had wanted or hoped. As Gitlin put it about the media coverage of the New Left in the 1960s: "Yet while they constrict and deform movements, the media do amplify the issues which fuel these same movements; . . . they expose scandals in the State and in the corporations, while reserving to duly constituted authority the legitimate right to remedy evils. The liberal media quietly invoke the need for reform—while disparaging movements that radically oppose the system that needs reforming" (1980, 4). Almost thirty years later, David Graeber echoes Gitlin almost exactly in his account of media coverage of antiglobalization activism: "One began to see editorials in *Time* and *Newsweek* claiming that anti-globalization protesters had been right all along. . . . Many seem to have lifted their arguments directly from activist op-ed submissions those same papers had refused to run. Clearly, these messages did have an effect. Yet one thing remained constant throughout: at no point were activists or activist intellectuals quoted, or allowed to use the mainstream press as a means to make these points themselves" (2009, 444).

For a more extended example, media scholar David Armstrong provides an entire chapter on the evolution of media coverage of the Vietnam War. He presents a detailed account of the back-and-forth movement between mainstream media representations, initially complicit with official information; alternative media coverage, challenging those representations; and eventual mainstream media turnaround with respect to the war. Late in the war, after the mainstream media had largely come around to the oppositional position, the antiwar documentary *Hearts and Minds* (1974) won an Academy Award for Best Documentary, "a development that would have been unthinkable," writes Armstrong, "in the early days of resistance to the war, before the underground media message softened up public opinion" (1981, 108). We will see a very similar history when we look at the relationship between Brave New Films' documentary campaign, and mainstream media coverage, regarding the twenty-first-century war in Afghanistan. In neither case can the alternative media claim to have stopped the war, which indeed went on for many years beyond the initial shifts in reporting. But in both cases a credible claim can be made for prodding and mobilizing the vast powers of the mainstream media and eventually having some effect.

If it is hard to overstate the power of mainstream media to shape much of what we know and feel about the world around us, it equally hard to overstate the importance of alternative media in not only telling the truth but also putting pressure on mainstream media to do so. I do not think it is an exaggeration, especially in the present era of the growth of right-wing extremism, to see alternative media as one of the primary lines of defense against the possibility of totalitarian governance in the United States and, indeed, most other parts of the world. In the next chapter, I turn to Brave New Films' own modes of truth-telling.

2 Critical Agency

THE POWER OF TRUTH

The truth will set you free, but first it will piss you off!
FEMINIST ICON GLORIA STEINEM

I began writing this book in the era of Donald Trump's presidency. There were many casualties of that regime, but one of them, as has been widely recognized, was the truth. Trump seemed to have no regard for the truth and no shame when he was shown to be—as was routinely the case— lying. Trump also popularized the phrase *fake news*, applying it to any story that showed him in a bad light, no matter how factually accurate or obviously true it might have been. Thus we are in what has come to be called a "post-truth" era, in which not only truth but often what counts as reality itself have been called into question.[1]

Now, as I write the present draft, Trump is out of office, but the extreme right-wing political movement that he praised and fueled is still with us and still wielding the weapons of lying, accusing all their enemies and crit-ics of lying, and more generally undermining the conceptual stability and comprehensibility of what most of us think of as the "real world." The most immediate casualty, and here I use the term *casualty* in its literal, physical sense, is the ongoing massive death count of the COVID pandemic, as the post-truth people have continued to refuse vaccination and to spread lies and sow confusion and ignorance about it, among other things.

While the problem of lying and cover-ups at the highest levels of government is long-standing, if not endemic (see Arendt 1969; Rosenfeld 2019), we seem to be in a particularly bad period of it at present, starting—as sketched earlier—in the year 2000 with the illegalities of the Bush-Cheney election. At the same time, we have ongoing problems in the mediascape, with the right-wing media amplifying the lies, and the mainstream media not doing enough to counteract them. Here, then, is where the value of the recent surge of political documentaries, with their commitment to showing and telling the truth, comes to the fore: "With the rise of 'fake news'—lies passing as fact—[documentaries] now seem to stand ever further apart from the mess of the news media. They are different. They remain on their truthful perch, albeit precariously" (Nick Fraser 2019, 341).

In the first sections of this chapter, I will provide an overview of the truth issue with respect to documentary film in general, and Brave New Films in particular. In the second part I will look at a range of BNF films to consider the different kinds of truth they seek to show and tell. Specifically, I will distinguish between truth-telling as challenging the lies and cover-ups of people in power, and truth-telling as revealing the deeper structural arrangements that reproduce injustice over time. Both kinds of truth-telling contribute, in different ways, to the production of what I am calling "critical agency," an aspect of agency grounded in the pursuit of factual knowledge about, and a clear understanding of, the dynamics of power and inequality.

Truth and the Documentary

The documentary film is by definition about truth. As film studies scholar Charles Musser has pointed out, the word *truth* has been part of virtually every major movement in the history of documentary, "from the US-based Veriscope ('truth viewer' in Latin) in the late 1890s to Dziga Vertov's *kino pravda* ('film truth' in Russian) in the 1920s and *cinéma vérité* ('truth cinema' in French) in the 1960s" (Musser 2007, 9). Or, as historian Paula Rabinowitz wrote, the documentary "poses truth as a moral imperative" (1994, 18).

If truth is the definitive goal and the moral imperative of documentary filmmaking, it is also subject to endless debate. What does it mean to be truthful in making a documentary film? Every filmmaker knows that making a film involves choices about shooting and editing (and more) that ultimately create the "truth" the film seeks to tell or show or reveal. How many and what kinds of choices are legitimate, and what kinds cross the line? Where is the line?

The debate is very old, going back almost to the beginning of the genre. It continues today, both in the work of film scholars (e.g., Gross, Katz, and Ruby 1988; Winston 1995) and in the criticism and self-criticism of documentary filmmakers themselves, who are always obsessing about the ethics of their own work and the work of others. In a useful article in *Filmmaker* magazine, we can see some of this range. The article opens with legendary filmmaker Haskell Wexler (*Medium Cool*, 1969) shouting, "Look, it's all fiction!" (Johnson 2007, 90) and ends with earnest comments by Sam Green, the codirector of *Weather Underground* (2002): "I do feel there are certain kinds of truth that are important for society. Those kinds of truths were ignored in the run up to the Iraq war, and look what happened. The postmodern idea that there is no truth, I don't agree with that, and it can lead to terrible things. There are things that are true, and the stakes are really high" (quoted in Johnson 2007, 107).

This is not the place for an extended discussion of the debate. By now I think most scholars accept the notion that truth is, as Foucault (e.g., [1977] 1980) and others have insisted, always historically and culturally relative and contingent. The question left open by Foucault's and similar formulations, however, is whether there is nonetheless some important sense, some remainder as it were, in which truth remains tied to some objective reality. Thus Bill Nichols, in his groundbreaking work on documentary, resists the formulation that "documentary is a fiction like any other" (1991, xi). Instead, he argues, "like other discourses of the real, [it] retains a vestigial responsibility to describe and interpret the world of collective experience" (1991, 10). Linda Williams, more committed to a Foucauldian view of truth as "contingent and relative" (1998, 381–82), nonetheless also argues for retaining some notion of the real. It is worth quoting her in full:

Truth [in documentary] is not "guaranteed" . . . yet some kinds of partial and contingent truths are nevertheless the always receding goal of the documentary tradition. Instead of careening between idealistic faith in documentary truth and cynical recourse to fiction, we do better to define documentary not as an essence of truth but as a set of strategies designed to choose from among a horizon of relative and contingent truths. The advantage, and the difficulty, of this definition is that it holds on to the concept of the real—indeed, of a "real" at all—even in the face of tendencies to assimilate documentary entirely into the rules and norms of fiction. (1998, 386)

While the association of documentary film and truth, and the debate over what that means and how it works, goes back a long way, it has become a more urgent issue in recent times, for real-world reasons discussed earlier. It almost seems as if every recent book about documentary film has the word *truth* in its title: *Shooting the Truth: The Rise of American Political Documentaries* (McEnteer 2006); *Crafting Truth: Documentary Form and Meaning* (Spence and Navarro 2011); *Speaking Truths with Film: Evidence, Ethics, Politics in Documentary* (Nichols 2016b); *Where Truth Lies: Digital Culture and Documentary Media after 9/11* (Fallon 2019). There are many articles as well, including Linda Williams's "Mirrors without Memories: Truth, History, and *The Thin Blue Line*" just quoted, and Toby Miller's "The Truth Is a Murky Path: Technologies of Citizenship and the Visual" (1998), but I will stop here and turn to Brave New Films.

Brave New Films and Documentary Truth

Like all documentary filmmakers, the people at Brave New Films are deeply invested in telling the truth with their films. For example, Devin Smith, vice president of operations, was talking about how he came to be doing this kind of work and how he came to be working for Brave New Films. Earlier he had been involved with the independent film scene, working on narrative (fiction) films. He had also interned for Robert Greenwald when Greenwald was still making movies for commercial TV. He then worked with Greenwald on *Uncovered: The Whole Truth about the Iraq War* (2004). He described working on that film as "an eye-opening experience for me," including interviewing CIA officers who were "concerned about telling the truth." When that project was finished, Greenwald invited him to stay on. He agreed in part because "he fell in love with the truth-telling quality of documentaries" (field notes, August 6, 2019).

Devin was using the word *truth* in the sense of the reality behind the official lies. Omar Samad, a coproducer at the company, used *truth* (and also *honesty*) in a slightly different sense, but with equal passion. When I first met him in his editing room, he was on the phone with someone about a new film he was making for the Brave New Films series *Following Their Lead: Youth in Action*. This is a series about high school students starting various activist projects. This particular film is about a seventeen-year-old young woman named Emily Weinberg who had started a movement for getting mental health included in high school health curricula. Omar explained after he got off the phone that the person at the other end (probably a freelance cameraperson) was afraid things might not work out, because it appeared that not enough people would show up for the demonstration they were hoping to film. Omar was very emphatic about going ahead anyway. As he said to me afterward, "We don't need a lot of people at the demo, we just need to see some action. What we want is *honesty*. People are trying to change something. It's hard to do activist work—that's the story." He continued: "We're making a documentary, we want to *tell the truth*. And we want Emily to be as *honest* as possible. So if she runs into roadblocks for her movement, that's part of the story" (field notes, June 7, 2019; emphasis in the original).[2]

Since 2002, Brave New Films has made eleven full-length documentary films, two shorter (thirty-eight minutes) documentaries, and virtually countless short videos, all strongly critical of a range of American policies and actions. Greenwald does not try to cover all the major political bases. There is very little about environmental issues, Indigenous issues, women/gender/patriarchy, and so forth. Rather, he concentrates on three broad areas of what might be called the perversion of American democracy—capitalism, racism, and (incipient) fascism—trying to show us truths about these things that we cannot learn from the mainstream media.

Further, Brave New Films puts truth-telling in the service of an explicitly activist agenda. As discussed earlier, the films are designed to get people activated politically, to get them up and out and doing the work of social justice. The films do this partly by arousing strong feelings about the injustices they show and explain. But they are not designed to appeal purely to emotions, to get people mindlessly fired up with anger and hate, even though the issues in the films are often infuriating and hateful. Rather they are designed to show and tell the truth, and thereby to promote activism based as much as possible on a clear understanding of the issues. I will discuss the affective side of the BNF film/political experience in chapter 4, and I recognize the artificiality of dividing the two dimensions of what is a single, complex whole. Here, however, I am trying to bring out the more analytical side of the process, and the production of what I am calling "critical agency."

An Aesthetic of Honesty

If we accept that truth in documentary is always constructed, even while it remains in some sense true, then we must begin by looking at the strategies of that construction. The first element of that process for Brave New Films has been widely noted: Greenwald's use of a very unadorned style of representation. Charles Musser describes *Uncovered* (about the invasion of Iraq) as having a "no-frills approach"; he also notes that there is a "poverty of production values," which is to say, of technical perfection and stylistic flourishes, and that these are all part of the film's "aesthetics of honesty" (Musser 2007, 15). In their discussion of *Outfoxed* (about Fox News), film scholars Ronald V. Bettig and Jeanne Lynn Hall write that the film "wears its low production values like a badge of honor and equates Fox [News'] flashy graphics and bombastic music with exploitative sensationalism and sanctimonious patriotism" (Bettig and Hall 2008). Film scholar Kris Fallon extends this point to Greenwald's films in general: "Like much of Greenwald's documentary output, *Outfoxed* works within a bare-bones style that offers little in the way of aesthetic flourish or formal innovation" (2019, 66). In sum, this bare-bones or no-frills style, which is partly an effect of working on a tight budget, is also a kind of statement of commitment to honesty and truth, as if to say, "We are not going to dazzle the viewer with fancy camerawork, splashy graphics, and attention-getting music. We are going to tell it like it is."[3]

A similar point, I would suggest, is made through the organizational and structural aspects of BNF films, which are straightforward in a different way: they are rigorously organized around a central theme, and they develop an argument through this rigorous organization. Described by one scholar as "methodically and consistently constructed" (Mackey-Kallis 2008, 169), many of them are built up through a series of named chapters, and even a list of questions to be addressed within each chapter, all carefully shown in panels on the screen. *Uncovered* (2004) displays this chapter structure ("Experts"; "Terrorism"; "Informers"; "Sixteen Words"; "Powell's Address to the U.N."; etc.). Some of the chapters are about the lies of the administration, some are about the debunking of the lies by the experts, some are about the war itself, and so forth. The film is complex, and Greenwald clearly wants to make sure that viewers can follow the argument and understand the issues at stake.

We see the same strategy in his recent film, *Suppressed: The Fight to Vote* (2019). Again the film has a series of chapters ("Polling Places"; "Registration"; "Purge"; "Absentee Ballots"; "Election Day"; and so forth). For the most part each chapter designates a different way voter suppression is being put into action. Here it is not so much that the film is complex and potentially hard to follow. Rather, the issue is that voter suppression operates through a large number of different kinds of mechanisms, some quite overt and some quite subtle, and again Greenwald wants this to be as clear as possible so the viewer can take it all in and process it.[4]

Finally, there is the frequent and repeated use of statistics. In every film we see individuals recounting their personal experiences, or expressing their expert opinions, or in other ways speaking from their own individual point of view. At the same time, virtually every film shows statistics on the screen in relation to what is being said, so that we know these individuals are not random examples or unique cases but instead represent much larger patterns. In *Making a Killing: Guns, Greed, and the NRA*, for example, we learn from panels on the screen that "33,636 Americans were killed by guns in 2013" and that "women are 500% more likely to be murdered if their abuser has a gun."

All of this represents a particular approach to political mobilization that puts significant emphasis on the cognitive and intellectual side of the process. While Greenwald certainly wants to rouse people to action, he does not simply want them to get irrationally pumped up in the manner of a Trump-style rally. In this respect his implicit position as a filmmaker strongly resonates with arguments made by Paulo Freire about political consciousness-raising in general: Freire insists on the importance of what he calls "reading the world" as part of progressive political action, as opposed to those "people [who] want less politics, less talk, and more results" and who denounce critical analysis as so much "blah-blah-blah." On the contrary, he says, "the constant exercise of 'reading the world,' requir[es] . . . a critical understanding of reality" (2004, 16–17).

I turn then to the contents of the films, starting with a group of films about lying itself, and the consequences of various kinds of falsification on the part of powerful actors.

Films about Truth I: Lying, Covering Up, and Sowing Confusion

Greenwald's first film as a director for Brave New Films was *Uncovered: The War on Iraq* (2004).[5] The film is a virtual textbook on criminal lying at the highest level of the American government. It details at great length the series of lies the Bush administration told to justify going to war against Iraq, and presents an equally detailed series of rebuttals by experts—CIA analysts, CIA operatives, high-level State Department officials—who were in a position to know the truth. Among other things, in the course of the run-up to the invasion, an inspection team was sent to Iraq to search for "weapons of mass destruction" (WMDs) supposedly being developed and stockpiled by the Iraqi government; the purported existence of these weapons served as one of Bush's major rationales for going to war. But when the inspection team found nothing, they and their findings were disparaged and dismissed. In the film, the leader of the team, David Kay, is clearly angry and says on-screen, "I'm a Republican and a fairly conservative person, but I don't let my ideology get in the way of the facts."

Brave New Films returned to this theme of blatant presidential lying in relation to Donald Trump. Trump's almost nonexistent commitment to truth takes several different forms. One is simply lying about anything and everything. BNF started a video series called *Trump vs. Trump*, in which Trump is shown repeatedly and egregiously contradicting himself. In *Trump vs. Trump on Putin and Russia*, for example, we see him describing his warm relationship with Putin in one series of screens, followed by another in which he literally says that he has never met Putin and does not know him. More recently, and more fatally, in *Trump vs. Trump on Coronavirus*, we hear Trump saying in the early stages of the pandemic that everything is fine and it will all go away. In the later stages he begins to backpedal, but when challenged by a reporter he reverts to insisting that his team is doing a great job and it will all be over soon. Here it is not so much a question of "lying," as in not telling the truth, but of an almost complete denial of objective reality, for which many have now paid with their lives.

A variant of high-level dishonesty involves cover-ups of official malfeasance. *War on Whistleblowers: Free Press and the National Security State* (2013) takes the perspective of several government employees who uncover government wrongdoing and try to tell the truth about it. The film begins with a series of images of important whistleblowers of recent times, including Daniel Ellsberg of the Pentagon Papers, Mark Felt ("Deep Throat") of the Watergate investigation, and Sherron Watkins of the Enron story. It follows the separate cases of four midlevel government bureaucrats who discover official wrongdoing, including knowingly sending fatally inadequate equipment to the American forces in Iraq, knowingly acquiring fatally flawed equipment for the coast guard, and illegally spying on the American citizenry. They try to tell the truth: they report these discoveries to their superiors, only to be told to keep quiet. After multiple efforts to right the wrongs through official channels, they go public as whistleblowers, theoretically a legally protected role serving the public interest. In all cases they lose their jobs and are harassed by criminal charges; three of them have had their lives more or less destroyed in the process.

Finally, let us consider one of BNF's best-known films, *Outfoxed: Rupert Murdoch's War on Journalism* (2004).[6] The film is about Fox News, the right-wing television channel owned by the Murdoch media empire that puts out a steady stream of ultraconservative programming while claiming (in its early years) to be "fair and balanced." Although it is no longer news that Fox News is not in fact "fair and balanced," the film remains highly relevant to the current situation insofar it provides a brilliant demonstration of the endless stream of, as one journalist put it, "distortion, misrepresentation, and sometimes outright fabrication" of what is supposed to be news and information, beamed out to millions of Fox viewers all day, every day. Going further, Greenwald learned from leaked internal memos that the lies and distortions were both systematic and coordinated—that the Fox leadership sends down daily memos about what should and should not be reported, and even about the language to be used in reporting (e.g., American military specialists shooting from rooftops should not be called "snipers," which has a negative connotation; rather, they should be referred to as "sharpshooters").

And then there is the manner in which Fox interviewers address their guests, including both the experts who appear on the news and the guests who appear in the interview segments. The hosts simply do not tolerate disagreement, and will shout at, berate, and verbally abuse anyone who tries to tell what they see as the truth of the situation under discussion. The most shocking case in the film is an interview with Jeremy Glick, whose father was killed in the attack on the World Trade Center on September 11, 2001, but who nonetheless later signed an antiwar petition protesting the invasion of Iraq. Interviewer Bill O'Reilly visibly lost his temper, repeatedly shouted at Glick, cut off his mike, and called security to escort him out of the studio.

As the treatment of Glick suggests, the Fox News hosts can win the argument every time, as they control the material situation—the mike, the security guard, and so on. But as one journalist in the film said, "Fox and conservatives don't have to win every argument. If they can muddy the argument enough, if they can turn it into a draw, that to them is a victory because it denies the other side a victory." I would go further here and suggest that the "muddying of the argument" is semi-intentional, part of a process of what has come to be called "gaslighting," of creating general confusion and murkiness, not only about who is right and wrong but also what is true and real.

Fox News does not have the official and legal powers of the president of the United States or the head of the National Security Agency. But as part of the media, and indeed an extremely influential part, its lies and distortions and fabrications can also have enormously powerful cultural effects. They contribute to the production and maintenance of what Antonio Gramsci (1971) called the "hegemonic order," our sense of reality specifically as it is conditioned/distorted by the worldview and values of the dominant sectors of society. Another aspect of the truth-work of BNF films is to try to disrupt and deconstruct that hegemonic order with their films, as I discuss in the next section.

Films about Truth II: Revealing "the Systemic"

Beyond the "aesthetics of honesty" in filmmaking practices, and beyond the films that make lying their subject matter, Greenwald approaches all of his subjects with a particular definition of truth that is captured by the term *systemic*. He has repeatedly said he is not interested in simply showing the viewer that, say, Walmart exploits its employees. That is true, and the *Wal-Mart* film does show that, but it is not, as it were, the whole truth. The whole truth is captured by showing—in probably the most important word in the BNF lexicon—that what Walmart is doing is "systemic," part of the larger unjust system we call capitalism, in which the exploitation of employees is built into the very nature of the business. As Greenwald said in an online interview, "We tell the story so people can connect the dots, so they understand how systemic so many of these things are. How they are rooted in the nature of capitalism and how the system works" (BNS_Robert_Greenwald_Discussions). Or as he said at the Los Angeles premiere of *Suppressed*, "We try to do 'systemic work,' about how specific cases are not just about themselves but about the system." Then he added, referring to the subject of *Suppressed*, "There is nothing more systemic than voting rights" (field notes, October 4, 2019).

The importance of showing the systemic nature of any given social issue is a deeply held value among Brave New Films staff. I sat in on another meeting in which BNF's director of production at the time, Justin Harrison, was working on ideas for a new film on the hidden costs of misdemeanor laws in relation to communities of color. Trying to be helpful, I mentioned that I had been reading James Forman's *Locking Up Our Own: Crime and Punishment in Black America* (2017), where the main point of the book is that the problem of criminalizing Black youth has continued even though police forces have become more integrated. Justin seemed to find the point useful because, as he said, "it goes to the 'systemic' nature of the problem" (field notes, June 7, 2019). Or in the conversation discussed earlier about Emily's campaign for including mental illness in high school health curricula, Omar said, "Emily is fighting for 'systemic change.'" He explained that Emily was not only lobbying for this issue in her own school but also drumming up support for pending state legislation to address the problem. He said that when he pitched the film to Greenwald, he emphasized the push for the legislation because that constitutes "systemic change" (field notes, June 7, 2019).[7]

Greenwald and the BNF staff are using "systemic" in the same way the #BlackLivesMatter movement uses it when, for example, they talk about police brutality. Police brutality, even to the point of death, must be understood not simply as the action of a few "bad apples" among the police but as a manifestation of a much wider and more deeply rooted problem: systemic racism, racism that is built into multiple institutional forms as well as into the habitus of white Americans more generally.[8] The term *systemic* here does not simply indicate that the problem is widespread, although that is an important element. It also, crucially, emphasizes the idea that the system contains an inherent bias, that it is weighted or rigged in a certain direction to produce the same bad outcomes over and over again.

The idea of "the systemic" thus specifies another kind of truth that Brave New Films pursues. This involves disrupting the hegemonic order, which renders exploitation invisible and seemingly unchangeable. It seeks to reveal the system of connections that lies beneath the visible harms and injustices, linking them together, tilting them in favor of existing structures of power, and continually reproducing them over time.

In the following section, then, I will look at some BNF films and videos with an eye toward the ways they make "the systemic" visible. I will organize the discussion by following the three major themes that are threaded, in different mixes, through all of BNF's films: corporate/neoliberal capitalism; racism and xenophobia; and the right-wing war on civil rights and democratic governance.

Capitalism as Systemic

Brave New Films shows again and again that capitalism is an amoral system that consistently puts profit over human well-being and human lives. The point is very basic, but it is easily ignored/forgotten/repressed as mainstream media celebrate the exploits of the rich and powerful and in other ways fail to ask critical questions about the harmful workings of the system. Brave New Films wants to remind its viewers of this very basic point in the most forceful way.

Greenwald often discusses the systemic bias of the capitalist economy using a language of "greed," of how corporate owners seek maximum profits regardless of the cost to others, and regardless of the fact that they already have more money than they could ever need or use. For example, in *Wal-Mart: The High Cost of Low Price* (2005), we are shown the deeply destructive effects of bringing a Walmart store into a community. The business is exploitative in the extreme, lowering wages below the poverty level and depressing entire local economies. And yet—as the film tells us, over images of their mansions and private jets—the Walton family that owns the company ranks among the top ten wealthiest families in the United States, and also ranks among the lowest in terms of philanthropic giving. A similar story is told in *Making a Killing: Guns, Greed, and the NRA* (2016). The film shows us all the terrible violence people do with guns, from domestic violence to gang warfare and mass shootings. The gun manufacturers, whose wealth is here again signaled in the film by pictures of their mansions—resist any and all kinds of regulation, all in the name of profit. Finally, *Unmanned: America's Drone Wars* (2013) shows the horrific effects of the American use of drone warfare in the Afghanistan region. Although the drones were touted as more precise in targeting "terrorists," in fact their use was expanded through the idea of "signature strikes" (targeting anyone who fits a "terrorist profile"), and the killing became almost random. A newscaster asks, "Who's cashing in on putting drones in the skies?" and a list of major American defense contractors with dollar amounts scrolls up the screen.

The theme of corporate greed continues in another set of films, but in the context of a slightly different point. These are films about formerly state functions that have now been privatized, turned into profit-making enterprises. While privatization of former state and public entities is now widespread in the American economy as a result of neoliberal economic policies, Greenwald's examples are drawn from the particularly violent realms of warfare and carceral punishment. One is a film called *Iraq for Sale: The War Profiteers* (2006), which focuses on the privatization of many functions of the US military during the Iraq War, where big private contractors like Halliburton and Blackwater basically ran the war as a for-profit, corporate operation. We learn about the many ways that these and other companies ignored the well-being, and sometimes cost the lives, of both the soldiers and their own civilian employees out of transparent profit-seeking motives.

Privatization of formerly federal, state, or municipal operations is also a central theme of a number of BNF videos on jails, prisons, and detention centers: *California's Punishment Economy: The State's $20 Billion Industry*; *Prison Profiteers: Six Institutions That Profit from the Police State*; and *Immigrant Prisons*. All of these short videos connect the ballooning of prison populations not only to racist and anti-immigrant policies and practices (discussed further below) but also to the conversion of the entire penal system into a major profit-making enterprise. Prisons, like wars, have become opportunities for legally making vast amounts of money, an incentive for expanding both with no end in sight.

Finally, capitalist greed, and disregard for human life or well-being, is the subject of *Koch Brothers Exposed* (2012), about the billionaire Koch brothers and their many destructive projects. More than the other films just discussed, this one shows the conversion of money into power, as the Koch brothers aggressively deploy their wealth in conservative political projects. I will have more to say about this film in the section on the subversion of democracy below, but the relevant point for now is the blatant environmental pollution generated by their industries, as we see whole communities literally poisoned downstream from their factories, while they spend millions lobbying against environmental regulation.

Racism and Xenophobia as Systemic

The second area of massive systemic bias that BNF takes on in their films is that of racism broadly conceived, including specifically anti-Black racism, as well as a broader spectrum of racial bias against all groups not considered white native-born Americans. The systemic point is again simple and basic: that racism is not just about personal prejudice, and not just about conservative "red states" or men in white hoods, but instead is deeply and widely woven throughout the entire fabric of American society.

Starting with racism specifically against African Americans, Brave New Films has focused primarily on the profound skewing of the criminal justice system, the many ways the entire system is racially rigged. For example, in *Prison System by the Numbers*, we are shown—in BNF's characteristically systematic way—how African American men are more likely to be punished by the criminal justice system at every step of the process: more likely to be arrested for minor crimes; if arrested, more likely to be convicted; and if convicted, more likely to receive longer sentences. At every step of the way, the proportion of African American individuals captured by the system increases, in the end producing the gross racial imbalance of American jails and prisons.

Second, other videos explain various specific mechanisms that drive this process. One is racial profiling, which is guaranteed to produce racial bias in arrest rates, as at the beginning of the chain just described (DEA *Boss to Agents: Target Black Neighborhoods, Avoid White Suburbs*). Another is mandatory sentencing for crimes, mostly drug related, which requires judges to impose often lengthy sentences, whether or not they believe such sentences are warranted (e.g., *Time to Come Home: 20 Years Is Enough: End Life Imprisonment*). Another is the plea bargain system, in which innocent people are persuaded to plead guilty if they cannot afford bail and are desperate to get out of jail (e.g., *Prisoner Gets a Bad Bargain: A Deal with the Devil*). Next there is the money bail system itself, which allows arrestees to get out of jail pending trial, but only if they can raise enough money to post bail. This system is transparently biased against poor people in general, and against Black people (because of the higher rates of arrest) in particular (e.g., *Breaking Down Bail: Debunking Common Bail Myths*; *The Bail Trap: American Ransom*).

Third, other videos explain the impact of all this on the African American community. For example, *A Deal with the Devil* tells the story of a man who steals a honey bun from a convenience store and is arrested. He is persuaded to take a plea deal, which includes one count of felony theft. The film goes on to show how a normal life becomes virtually impossible after a felony conviction, and details all the benefits and rights such a person may lose after the conviction: "social benefits, voting rights, jury duty, education benefits, parental rights, travel rights, employment rights, housing benefits."

Turning then to the treatment of refugees, asylum seekers, and immigrants, there are always certain groups—which have varied over the course of American history—that are treated as racially despised others and subjected to violent abuse. One such group, in the current Trumpian racist imaginary, is "Mexicans"—in other words, any Latin American person who seeks to enter the United States via the border with Mexico. For example, in *Meet the Nazis That Patrol the U.S.-Mexico Border*, an interviewer talks with one Harry Hughes, who represents an organization calling itself National Socialists, and who proudly wears the swastika. Harry sees his job as capturing refugees crossing the border, whom he describes as "disposable," as "throwaway people." The point of the film is that Harry is not simply some delusional individual, but that people like Harry are driving the broader rhetoric and policies of immigration. Addressing the audience, the tagline of the film makes the systemic point: "If you don't speak up, they will speak for you."

Other films in this group emphasize the extraordinary brutality of the law enforcement agencies at the US-Mexico border. *Families Torn Apart: America's Deadly Immigration Policy* begins with a warning that everything we will see is true, and viewer discretion is advised; the film is indeed very painful to watch. It begins with close-ups of crying children's faces, with a soundtrack of continuous crying in the background; the middle section shows parents and children reuniting, with weeping parents and the number of days of separation shown on the screen, some as much as one year; and the final section begins with the title "These children will never be reunited with their parents" and shows a long series of snapshots of children who died in detention.

The films just discussed focus on the often hidden and invisible mechanisms by means of which racism is enacted, perpetuated, and rendered systemic. They help us understand racism "in itself," as it were, as a pernicious system of hatred and violence directed against racialized and demonized others. In addition, however, racism plays a large role as a weapon in the politics of would-be totalitarian governance, to which we now turn.

Fascism as Emergent: The War on Democratic Governance

Capitalism and racism in the United States are as old as the nation itself. Arguably, capitalism has gotten more extreme in recent years with the abandonment of any kind of social agenda under neoliberal theory and practice. Arguably, racism too has grown more extreme, or at least more blatant, under both neoliberal governance and the Trumpist right-wing agenda. But the visible growth of violent right-wing extremism is a relatively recent phenomenon, with right-wing groups growing in numbers and, more importantly, in a sense of legitimacy and empowerment, as they have been encouraged to act out by Trump (whether in or out of office), by some Republican legislators, and by wealthy backers (see Mayer 2016; MacLean 2017; Neiwert 2017). The most recent and shocking manifestation of this took place as I was working on this chapter. On January 6, 2021, a large and violent right-wing mob breached the gates, climbed the walls, and stormed the US Capitol to disrupt the certification of the presidential election. Thugs paraded around in the Senate chamber carrying Confederate flags and wearing Nazi T-shirts. Shots were fired and several people were killed.

Brave New Films has been tracking various aspects of this process, from their very first film, *Unprecedented* (2002), about the highly controversial Bush/Gore presidential election, to their most recent film, *Suppressed* (2019), about the widespread practice of voter suppression. Insofar as they are attempting to disrupt a particular hegemonic configuration, that configuration is complacency about the American democratic system, and a failure to recognize the degree to which the country is tilting in the direction of fascism.

But the language and style of the films with respect to this issue are somewhat different from those just discussed. Whereas BNF takes it for granted that both capitalism and racism are deeply "systemic," right-wing extremism and the attempted subversion of democracy are treated more as, in Raymond Williams's (1977) terms, "emergent," not yet "systemic," but nonetheless dangerous trends that must be recognized and resisted before it is too late.

More than half of Brave New Films' output since 2002 has been devoted to one or another aspect of this rightward shift. I would include in this group the films about high-level lying discussed earlier; we know from many accounts of totalitarianism, not least from the great novel *1984* (Orwell 1949), that the manipulation of truth and reality is central to such a regime.

Two other clusters of films in this category address more direct attempts to subvert American democracy, one focusing on the setting aside of civil rights in the name of security, and the other on the multipronged assault on the electoral system. All of these together begin to point in the direction of a state that, by many definitions, could be called fascist. Further, if these films on the erosion of democratic governance are put together with the films in the previous section—on the wars against any and all people defined as racial others—the picture of a growing fascism in America becomes even clearer: the combination of authoritarian governance and violence against racially dehumanized persons is one of the distinctive hallmarks of a fascist regime (see especially Stanley 2018; see also Paxton 2005; Griffin 1995; De Genova 2020).

I'll start with *Unconstitutional: The War on our Civil Liberties* (2004).[9] The film was sponsored by the American Civil Liberties Union (ACLU), and tells the story of the Patriot Act, crafted by the Bush II administration as part of the "war on terror" after the attacks on the World Trade Center in 2001. The film systematically presents the ways the powers of law enforcement were expanded, while many of the fundamental rights guaranteed by the US Constitution—especially surrounding due process of the law—were scrapped in the name of protecting the nation from terrorism. Although the main targets of the act were "terrorists," civil rights lawyers in the film explain that many parts of the act had nothing to do with terrorism and were simply opportunistic expansions of domestic spying.

It is worth mentioning *War on Whistleblowers* again here. I discussed this film above with respect to the "war on truth," as we saw government employees being punished for trying to tell the truth about serious forms of government malfeasance. But the other theme of that film is the exponential growth of the "national security" apparatus of the American state, of which the Patriot Act is only one element.

The ostensible purpose of the Patriot Act was the capture and punishment of "terrorists," which after 9/11, and viewed from a right-wing perspective, basically meant Muslims, or anyone who remotely even might be a Muslim—a person with a Middle Eastern name, a person wearing a turban, and so on. In fact, as we will see in other films in this section, many of the attempts to subvert democracy involve targeting one or another group of persons of color. But in the context of these particular films, the racist aspect is folded into the issue of subversion of democracy. Unlike the films about the more direct assaults on African Americans, immigrants, and other persons of color, discussed earlier, the films in this group emphasize how racism and xenophobia are mobilized in pursuit of a different goal: getting rid of constitutional constraints against the abuse of state power.

A different right-wing assault on civil liberties and democratic governance involves the manipulation of the electoral system, about which BNF has made two films. The first of these is *Unprecedented: The 2000 Presidential Election* (2002).[10] The film tells the story of all the chicanery involved in the presidential election of 2000, in which George W. Bush walked away with a highly contested victory over Al Gore. We learn about how the voter rolls were purged beforehand of mostly African American voters who were presumed to be voting Democratic. The election eventually came down to a recount that was interrupted first by some "demonstrators" who turned out to be a mob of Republican staffers, and then by the US Supreme Court, which, on very questionable legal grounds, stopped the recount again and handed the election to George W. Bush.[11]

Greenwald returned to the issue of voter suppression in 2019, with his film *Suppressed: The Fight to Vote* (2019).[12] The film tells a very similar story, this time of the 2018 Georgia gubernatorial race between Democrat Stacey Abrams and Republican Brian Kemp. Kemp was Georgia's secretary of state, and in that capacity he put in motion an expanded range of mechanisms designed to suppress the Democratic vote, including purging the voter rolls, putting many applications for voter registration "on hold," closing many polling places, not providing enough voting machines in key Democratic districts, and on and on. Again most of these measures largely affected African American voters. In the end Brian Kemp "won" by more than fifty thousand votes, although Stacey Abrams challenged the outcome in a very powerful speech in which she refused to concede and thereby to legitimate an illegitimate process.

Finally, in *Koch Brothers Exposed* (2012) we see how manipulation of the voting system is one part of a larger, ultraconservative agenda. In the film we meet Charles and David Koch, owners of a vast private empire of oil- and gas-related corporations.[13] The film takes us through a series of ultraconservative causes, programs, and groups the Koch brothers have financed with their money: the privatization of public schools, including an attempt to resegregate an integrated school system in Wake County, North Carolina; the defeat of national legislation for environmental regulation; the financing of the campaign of Scott Walker for governor of Wisconsin, and the backing of his successful drive to bust the public sector unions; and the backing of voter suppression legislation in many states designed to reduce the participation of presumed Democratic—mostly Black and minority—voters.[14]

Although the word *fascism* is never actually uttered in any of the films, it is clear that the developments they portray, especially when taken together, point in that direction, and several of the films contain fairly explicit warnings to think about the frightening implications of these trends. In the bonus material of *Unprecedented* there are several very strong warnings about an authoritarian takeover. Political scientist Frances Fox Piven calls the 2000 presidential election "a *coup d'état*, an illegal seizure of power to which the Supreme Court of the United States was a party." She continues, "It's quite frightening; we ought to be more frightened." And author Gore Vidal says, "I really sort of mark the end of the republic, that that election passed without much outcry."

Similarly, in a later video titled *Mental Health Experts and Donald Trump*, we hear a repeated language of "warning the public," of "alerting and warning everyone" about the risks of a presidency in the hands of someone like this president. One psychologist specifically says that he and other members of his field have an obligation to speak out today, that they cannot make the mistake German psychologists made of keeping silent while watching the rise of Hitler and fascism in the 1930s. By the time I write this, Trump is out of office, but the growth of right-wing extremism continues unabated.

I conclude this section by noting again the close intertwining of the attacks on democratic governance and the mobilization of racist campaigns, and by emphasizing again that the linkage between authoritarian governance and virulent racism is the particular hallmark of fascism. The films show clearly that the "war on terror" in the name of national security becomes the excuse for a war on "Muslims" and "immigrants"; the voter manipulation activities in the name of "voter fraud prevention" become the excuse for suppressing the votes of African Americans and other nonwhite minorities. And the two issues (and more) are closely joined in the ultraconservative agenda of the Koch brothers and virtually all right-wing groups.

This brings us to one more warning: the famous "Confession" by Lutheran pastor Martin Niemöller in Germany after World War II, which emphasizes that no one is safe under fascist rule, even the people who think they are safe because they are not members of one of those minorities they may despise. This text scrolls down the screen at the end of *Unconstitutional*:

> First they came for the Communists and I did not speak out because I was not a Communist;
> Then they came for the socialists and I did not speak out because I was not a socialist;
> Then they came for the trade unionists and I did not speak out because I was not a trade unionist;
> Then they came for the Jews and I did not speak out because I was not a Jew;
> Then they came for me and there was no one left to speak out for me.[15]

This is the first of three chapters on the ways Brave New Films seeks to cultivate in people a sense of political agency, a sense of the need for political action, and a sense of empowerment to take such action. In the present chapter I have focused on the cultivation of "critical agency," agency motivated by factual knowledge and critical understanding of issues. While recognizing the artificiality of dividing this off from questions of affect and emotion, I wanted to bring out the ways that BNF films, like all documentary films, are grounded in a commitment to "truth" in several senses—as a way of making their films, as a campaign against lying and dishonesty in government, and as the deconstruction of "hegemonic ignorance" perpetuated in part by both right-wing and mainstream media. Learning and embracing truth in these various senses is the basis of agency in its critical aspect.

But Brave New Films does not rely solely on the power of the films themselves to mobilize political activism. The company both draws from and contributes to a larger world of social justice work, to which we now turn.

3 Networked Agency

THE POWER OF THE SOCIAL

Democracy is not a spectator sport.
ROBERT GREENWALD

I opened this book with some sketches of the role of "powerful texts" in historical and ethnographic cases of radical social change. The nature of the texts is quite variable—the Bible and the newspaper appear to be very different things. What they have in common is that they are read by vast numbers of people across a wide swath of society, and they are seen as embodying some important form of truth, whether transcendental or mundane. It is at the intersection of those two points, where people get together and discuss the critical implications of those truths for the current state of the world they live in, that something called consciousness-raising can occur. Collectively with one another, and in relation to a text that opens up new vistas on the world, people may begin to feel the need and the inclination to take action.

In the previous chapter, I explored the range of BNF films and their various strategies of truth-telling. Like most political documentaries, BNF films pursue truth at multiple levels—in their making, in their subject matter, and in their concern for the deeper form of truth we call "systemic." In the present chapter I situate Brave New Films in the context of social movements, the complex arrangements through which people organize for social change. I look at the ways in which the films move through what film scholar Caty Borum Chattoo calls an "ecology of activism," thus extending and amplifying political agency through what might be called "the power of the social."

Movements, Culture, and "Vision"

The study of social movements extends across several disciplines, including sociology (e.g., Tarrow 2011; Goodwin and Jasper 2015), social and cultural history (e.g., Thompson 1963; Hill 1972; Eley 1992; Sewell 2005), and anthropology (e.g., Gibb 2001; Nash 2005; Juris and Khasnabish 2013; Theodossopoulos 2017).[1] I draw on all of these at one point or another in this work. The sociologists are particularly useful on the organizational aspects of movements, and I will come back to them at several points later in this chapter.

But the anthropologists, along with many culturally inclined historians, bring a strong emphasis on the cultural aspects of social movements, and I want to start with that here. "Our premise," write anthropologists Richard G. Fox and Orin Starn, "is that protest necessarily involves struggle over ideas, identities, symbols, and strategies . . . and we assert the inextricability of the culture of politics and the politics of culture" (1997, 3). Or, as anthropologists Sonia E. Alvarez, Evelina Dagnino, and Arturo Escobar write, "Culture is political because meanings are constitutive of processes that . . . seek to redefine social power. That is, when movements deploy alternative conceptions of woman, nature, race, economy, democracy, or citizenship that unsettle dominant cultural meanings, they enact a cultural politics" (1998, 7; see also Escobar 1992). My discussions in the previous chapter about BNF films seeking to disrupt the untruths and invisibilities of entrenched ("hegemonic") common sense were very much within that framework of "unsettling dominant cultural meanings."

Another major cultural aspect of social movements concerns the vision of the future that drives such movements. No movement is merely negative, merely oppositional. Every act of resistance, no matter how short-term and limited in immediate objectives, carries with it at the same time a vision of a better world. As anthropologists Igor Cherstich, Martin Holbraad, and Nico Tassi (2020) have emphasized, such visions are always culturally specific, formulated not only in reaction to local forms of inequality and injustice but also in relation to broader cultural notions of time, space, and personhood (see also Ortner 1995). Regardless of the specifics, however, some vision of a better world is at the heart of every social movement. Paulo Freire put particular emphasis on this aspect, asserting his "conviction that overcoming injustices . . . implies the articulated exercise of imagining a less ugly, less cruel world. It implies imagining a world we dream of, a world that is not yet, one different from the world that is, and a world to which we need to give form" (2004, 14). And again: "What is not possible . . . is to even think about transforming the world without a dream, without utopia, or without a vision" (2004, 31).

Many movements articulate their vision in some kind of manifesto or statement. Brave New Films offers a series of statements, on their website and in their annual reports, describing themselves and their work. They offer a "mission statement": "to champion social justice issues by using a model of media, education, and grassroots volunteer involvement that inspires, empowers, motivates and teaches civic participation and makes a difference." There is also a "vision statement": "Our vision is an open democratic society that encourages rigorous debate, opportunity, and justice for all."[2]

The BNF vision statement is particularly broad and open, and we need to turn to their films to get a more specific sense of what they hope to achieve. In doing so we get a more complex picture of their vision, which is not so much about a vague future society as about moments and pockets of our present world where "civic participation" and "an open democratic society" are actually realized in the present. Greenwald's films always include scenes of political participation, and particularly scenes of successful political participation. In other words, a central part of the vision is activism itself. At the conclusion of this chapter I will return to the films and look more closely at the vision of a better world that is embedded in them.

Documentary Film within an Ecology of Activism

There has recently been a spate of exciting work that looks at political documentary not only in terms of its content but also in terms of the ways it is socially and materially linked to activist politics on the ground. There has been earlier work on this subject, especially the histories of documentary production collectives like Kartemquin Films (Blumenthal and Rohrer 1980; Aguayo 2019) and Newsreel (Nichols [1972] 2016; Renov 2004). But every part of the documentary phenomenon has been expanded in recent times: there are more political films, there is more explicit acknowledgment of political intent, and there are more real-world ways of linking them to social movements on the ground. I begin, then, by running through some of the main themes of this newer work, which begins, like everything else in this book, in the wake of the crises at the turn of the twenty-first century.

We may start with media studies scholar David Whiteman's felicitously titled article "Out of the Theaters and into the Streets" (2004). Arguing against what he calls an "individualistic model" of interpreting documentary work, Whiteman calls for a "coalitional approach" to the study of political documentary. I quote him in full: "[This approach] (a) must conceptualize film as part of a larger process that incorporates both production and distribution (not simply as a 'product' for consumption); (b) must consider the full range of potential impacts on producers, participants, activist organizations, and decision makers (in addition to the typical focus on citizens); and (c) must consider the role of films in the efforts of social movements to create and sustain alternative spheres of public discourse (in addition to focusing on mainstream public discourse)" (2004, 51–52). In sum, the study of political documentary must situate it in social and political contexts at all stages of its life.

In *Documentary Resistance: Social Change and Participatory Media* (2019), Angela K. Aguayo makes a similar argument. Calling for a focus on "participatory media cultures," she argues, "By shifting focus from a traditional understanding of social change documentary—as a series of intentions and aesthetics—to look more broadly at how documentary engages political structure(s), our understanding of the scope and function of documentary's transformative potential expands" (2019, 6). Aguayo also takes this point in a somewhat different direction from Whiteman, putting greater emphasis on the ways that documentary work is often the product of community efforts: "Most social change documentary manifests locally, with community-based organizing and coalition building with other struggles, coalescing in participatory media cultures invested in change" (2019, 5).

For a third example we may look at Caty Borum Chattoo's *Story Movements: How Documentaries Empower People and Inspire Social Change* (2020). Borum Chattoo takes a similar position about the embeddedness of documentary in webs of social process and social institutions. In one chapter she discusses its role specifically in social movements, but her focus is on more general forms of "civic engagement" facilitated by documentary film and the "ecology" of institutions that support them: "This conceptualization of contemporary social-issue documentaries as civic storytelling positions the interplay among publics, civil society, media narratives, and the tools and conventions of contemporary activism. Documentary storytelling, in this context, is not a form of media content to passively consume but a nucleus of civic practice that empowers public engagement" (2020, 62).

The idea that a media form should be seen as both a product and a source of histories and institutions and social forces will not exactly be news for a social scientist. The difference for the present situation is that all of this is no longer simply a set of background conditions; it has been taken up quite intentionally in the world of documentary film and is now part of the conscious culture of documentary filmmaking. Filmmakers mobilize every kind of social support they can to make their films, and every strategy they can think of to enhance the probability of the film having social impact.

Cinema and media scholars agree that Brave New Films played a leading role in this development. Christian Christensen takes Brave New Films as an extended illustration for the value of Whiteman's "coalitional approach" (2009), and Caty Borum Chattoo opens *Story Movements* with an extended anecdote about Brave New Films' *Wal-Mart* (2004) and its use of a "coalition-based" approach (see also Smithline 2005). Borum Chattoo also pinpoints *Wal-Mart's* impact more specifically: "The Walmart documentary wasn't the first to leverage a coalition-based approach to raise awareness and mobilize publics around a social challenge. But the film was shaped and distributed in a meaningful juncture—in the crevasse between the early digital century and the looming revolution of the participatory networked media age" (2020, 3). And within Kris Fallon's *Where Truth Lies: Digital Culture and Documentary Media after 9/11* (2019) there is an entire chapter titled "Networked Audiences: MoveOn .org and Brave New Films," in which Fallon describes the collaboration between MoveOn and BNF as "one of the key historical moments in the remediation of nonfiction video and online political organizing" (2019, 14).

"When the film is finished," wrote Greenwald in a recent email, "our work just begins" (February 28, 2021). In this chapter, I move beyond the films themselves to situate the work of Brave New Films within the wider framework of the forms and mechanisms, both on the ground and digital, of social movements. I look ethnographically at, to adapt a phrase from Arjun Appadurai (1986), the social life of the films, the ways they are used to contribute to the formation of publics, networks, face-to-face groups—what we might think of as social movement infrastructure. I will look at three forms of work in this area: BNF's social media practices, their practices of "partnering" with other social justice organizations, and the system of promoting screenings of their films.

Social Media and the Construction of Counterpublics

Social media have become indispensable tools of political activism (Juris 2008; Juris and Khasnabish 2013). While they can serve many practical functions of organizing, connecting, and scheduling real on-the-ground groups and actions, they are most fully understood in this context as calling into being what political philosopher Nancy Fraser called "counterpublics." As part of a critique of the work of philosopher Jürgen Habermas, which emphasized a unified "bourgeois public sphere," Fraser argued that "members of subordinated social groups—women, workers, people of color, and gays and lesbians—have repeatedly found it advantageous to constitute alternative publics." She calls these "subaltern counterpublics," which she defines as "parallel discursive arenas where members of subordinated social groups invent and circulate counterdiscourses to formulate oppositional interpretations of their identities, interests, and needs" (1992, 123; see also Eley 1992). Here I consider BNF's social media operation as one site in which an oppositional, progressive, and racially diverse counterpublic is called into being and sustained, a loose assemblage of at least partially like-minded people, reflected most visibly in the numbers of hits and shares in response to social media posts. Just to be clear, this is not (yet) an activist group but, rather, a kind of pool from which such a group might be formed.

The Brave New Films social media operation is run by a social media manager who puts out content on all the social media platforms. The content will include clips from the most currently released film, both referring viewers to the full film and capturing highlights of the film for audiences who may never see the film itself. It might also include clips from an older film that has become relevant due to a specific event or occasion. Danielle Cralle, the social media manager at the time of my research, gave the example of *Making a Killing*, their film on gun violence: "So *Making a Killing*, our film on gun [violence], is still relevant today. And actually, on the 18th through the 20th [of July], that's the anniversary of the Aurora, Colorado, movie theater shooting. And so we're doing a mini campaign on that, just to remind people. We covered that extensively in our film, and it's to remind people that we still have such a long way to go. There are so many more actions we need to take" (interview, July 12, 2019).

In addition, BNF produces two-to-three-minute videos specifically for social media, meant to keep up with very current events. In the period leading up to the 2020 election, there were many videos to encourage voting, some of them new and made for that purpose, and others clipped from *Suppressed 2020*. There were also several increasingly critical short videos about Trump, some of which I discussed in the previous chapter.

This period also saw the beginning of the COVID-19 pandemic. Brave New Films produced a series of short videos on the pandemic, including several expressing appreciation for the health care and other essential workers, and several slamming Trump for his (non)handling of the pandemic. This included a three-part series called *A Preventable COVID Tragedy*, with each short video featuring a person who lost a close family member to the disease. One of these, *Maddie's Grandparents: A Preventable COVID Tragedy*, was picked up by several major media outlets, including CNN and MSNBC.

Social media is all about "reach." Currently BNF has an overall audience of roughly 500,000 on Facebook; 20,000 on Twitter plus 20,000 on Greenwald's personal Twitter;[3] 120,000 on YouTube; and almost 20,000 on Instagram. For any given post, the gross number of views is important, but more important is what they call "engagements": comments and shares. Shares—forwarding to others—are seen as particularly important. As Danielle put it, "If something has 252 shares, that means people are sharing it across their Messenger. That's impactful. That's something people are interested in" (interview, July 12, 2019). Again, the total number of people who see something is important, and big numbers can be very exciting. When *Suppressed 2020*, the updated version of *Suppressed*, premiered via Facebook, Robert Greenwald exulted, "270,000 people saw it yesterday!" (email, August 6, 2020). But the "sharing" expresses the more "social" dimension of "social media": "If somebody's sharing," Danielle said, "they're sharing it to someone they know, someone they're probably close to" (interview, July 12, 2019), making it more meaningful.

The cover of the *2020 Brave New Films and Brave New Films Action Fund Impact Report* consists entirely of statistics, in very large font, including a summary of their total social media reach for the past year: 19.6 million views and 1.4 million "engagements." These numbers may be seen as representing the full counterpublic that BNF calls into being, specifically through its social media. It is not in itself a social movement, and it is not even a social network (discussed in the next section). It is a collection of many people who share certain interests and who participate in a virtual counterpublic space where, in the words of activist anthropologist Jeffrey Juris, "oppositional identities, discourses, and practices are produced and through which they circulate" (2008, 201).

Beyond the aggregate numbers, each film draws an at least partially different public, related to the specific subject matter of the film.[4] In the case of *Suppressed*, for example, the public in question has a strong African American component, as will be visible in the discussions below. But other films will draw in other groups, and insofar as there is something like a generic Brave New Films counterpublic, it consists of quite a socially diverse body of people.

Partnering and the Production of Activist Networks

Although networks of activist groups and organizations are part of counterpublics, I break them out here as referring to people or groups between whom there are actual links, whether electronic or physical, as opposed to a collection of individuals whose only link is that they are all on the same social media list. Networks in this sense have always been part of social movement activism, although their expansion and maintenance has been enormously facilitated by the availability of electronic and digital media, especially email and web-based communication. They can be activated by movements in an activist phase to plan and coordinate movement events, as in Jeffrey Juris's account of the movement against corporate globalization, *Networking Futures* (2008). Juris not only documents these basic forms of network activity but also sees a larger progressive role for the network form, arguing that it embodies "an effective model for reorganizing society as a whole," including "open access, the free circulation of information, self-management, and coordination based on diversity and autonomy" (2008, 15, 16).

But the network is also important for sustaining ideas and relationships even when movements are not in phases of public activism. Sociologist Sidney Tarrow writes of "the *connective structures* or *interpersonal networks* that link leaders and followers, centers and peripheries, and different parts of a movement sector with one another, permitting coordination and aggregation, and allowing movements to persist even when formal organization is lacking" (2011, 124). Anthropologists Sonia Alvarez, Evelina Dagnino, and Arturo Escobar propose using the term *web* rather than network, as the term better captures "the multilayered entanglements of movement actors. . . . Movement webs encompass more than movements and their active members; they include occasional participants in movement events and actions, and sympathizers and collaborators in NGOs [nongovernmental organizations], political parties, universities, other cultural and conventionally political institutions, the Church, and even the state" (1998, 15–16).

The network idea is formalized, at least in the world of activist filmmaking, in the idea of "partnering." Partnering involves linking social justice filmmakers with relevant organizations with whom they might work in the filmmaking itself, and/or in the process of circulating the film and amplifying its impact afterward. Many documentary filmmakers, especially when they are starting out, may not have their own connections in activist networks, and nonprofit organizations have emerged to help them develop such connections. For example, an organization called Doc Society has a program called Good Pitch, which presents itself as follows: "We bring together documentary filmmakers with leading change makers around urgent social issues to forge new coalitions that are good for the films and good for society." They go on to present statistics: almost $33 million raised for films and impact campaigns, over 5,000 participating organizations, over 1,700 long-term partnerships brokered, and so forth.[5] Note the language of both "forg[ing] new coalitions" and "broker[ing] partnerships."

In the case of Brave New Films, Robert Greenwald was already involved in social justice work when he started the company, including having connections with the nascent (at the time) internet organizing group MoveOn.org. As discussed earlier, it was the partnership with MoveOn, and Eli Pariser's suggestion that they have screening parties in people's homes, that launched the model BNF still follows for its activism, including the reliance on both activist partnerships and live screenings.

A unique array of partners will be developed for each individual film, based on the film's subject matter. Some of these partnerships may carry over across a number of films insofar as certain themes reappear, as discussed in the previous chapter. The American Civil Liberties Union (ACLU) appears as a partner in quite a few BNF films, since many of those films are concerned with issues of democracy and civil liberties. Nonetheless, each film will also have its own partners for its specific issues and cases.

Some partnering begins at the point of production. For example, Executive Director Jim Miller, who had had a career in nonprofit work before coming to work for Brave New Films, has a large personal network of connections in some of the major national social justice NGOs. When BNF decides on a particular subject for a film, Miller will often kick off the process by contacting his connections in the relevant organizations, putting them in touch with the BNF production staff. Some of these connections in turn become ongoing partners in making the film: they act as consultants on the issues and help BNF find some of the people who appear in the film. Sometimes these partnerships work both ways. Miller told a story of getting a list of names for *Suppressed* from a lawsuit that Stacey Abrams's Fair Fight organization was bringing over the contested 2018 Georgia gubernatorial election. But as Miller gleefully recounted, the BNF production staff was so good at finding people that they were able to give the lawyers names they hadn't even found: "As it turned out, our production staff was even more adept than the folks that were putting together the lawsuit. We were able to find stories that they weren't able to find, which is really, really terrific!" (interview, June 24, 2019).

Some partnerships are basically event-oriented. A specific set of groups and individuals will be recruited to have their names listed as cosponsors for particular events. High-profile events (e.g., a film's premiere) will have more national-level sponsors and bigger-name individuals, while local events will have more local groups: for instance, a campus screening will have various campus groups as cosponsors. As one example of a mix of sponsors in what we might think of as a kind of midlevel event, when Pennsylvania state senator Art Haywood held a screening of *Suppressed 2020*, he listed the following partners: "Black Voters Matter, Committee of Seventy, Head Count, NAACP, Johnson House Historic Site Germantown, League of Women Voters of Philadelphia, and Uncle Bobbie's Coffee and Books."[6]

There are also "social media share partners," high-profile individuals (e.g., Robert Reich) or organizations that agree to share/forward each other's social media postings to their own lists.

But some of the largest numbers of partnerships are developed in relation to "outreach," the effort to get the film seen by the largest possible audience; MoveOn, as noted earlier, was the first such partner for BNF. This is the job of the outreach director, who is normally a person with a background in nonprofit and social justice work. (He or she may have some background in film, but that is not a requirement for the job.) Anne Phillips, the outreach director when I was doing the research for this project, had done community organizing in Texas and fundraising for several nonprofits (one of them national), and had also served as the executive director of what she described as a small, struggling nonprofit, before she came to Brave New Films.

Anne set an ambitious (and catchy) goal of signing up 2020 screenings of *Suppressed* (and later of *Suppressed 2020*) by the time of the presidential election in 2020. Screenings are generated in part through the Brave New Films website. Anyone can click on any film on the site and propose to hold a screening, and the outreach group will help them set it up. In addition, and more important in terms of numbers, the outreach director contacts major organizations and coalitions to see if they would be interested in promoting the film to their chapters and their membership lists. If so, they become "partners" in a more official sense, and Brave New Films will offer to tailor the film's end credits to display the organization's website and other contact information so, for example, "the ACLU can have their own version of *Suppressed* with their call to action at the end. Or the Indivisible chapters will have their call to action at the end" (interview, May 31, 2019).

Anne's approach to the job was entirely based on cultivating personal relationships with individuals in other organizations: "I got into the fundraising path for many years, and learned that relational approach. . . . It's really about investing in people and communities. If you're in love with the organization you're fundraising for, and other people are, then why not be in relation with one another?" (interview, May 31, 2019). She brought this approach to Brave New Films and spoke of developing relationships with various organizations and coalitions through "concentric circles" of connections. Much of this work takes place before the film is released, laying the groundwork for action when it comes out. And it is based as much as possible on cultivating relationships: "I ask," Anne said, "'Hey, how can this help you?' . . . I think with me as a relationship-building person, I want it to be helpful for them. I don't want to be pushing this onto them. [I ask,] 'Is this going to be useful [for you]?'" (interview, May 31, 2019).

This point about relationships is key to understanding that the linkages with other groups are not simply strategic, promoting the film and racking up big numbers of screenings, although that is one of the goals. It is also about developing and extending ties within the larger advocacy networks as an end in itself. For example, in one staff meeting Greenwald talked about making a short film about the Congressional Black Caucus. As I wrote in my notes at the time: "He has been talking to [Representative] Karen Bass [of California] about the Black Caucus in Congress. With its 57 members, it is the largest caucus in the House. It also has 5 [congressional] committee chairs. They discussed making a video showing all the work that's being done by the Black Caucus, and having a big gala premiere." (The film subsequently came out: *The CBC: Fighting for Black America*.) There was no immediate instrumental purpose or goal to doing this. Rather, Greenwald said, "it's all about building relationships." He looked around and repeated: "It's relationships, relationships, relationships" (field notes, June 7, 2019). In this sense, then, Brave New Films does not simply offer their films as tools of political persuasion, however powerful. They also both join and extend the larger network of activist groups that serves as the durable infrastructure of potential social movements.

Screenings

Screenings can reach a surprisingly large number of people. While the numbers from individual requests through the website may not be very large, the numbers increase geometrically when multiplied through networks of partners. Kris Fallon writes that "MoveOn's house-party event for . . . *Wal-Mart* . . . put together seven thousand simultaneous screenings. Arguably, it enjoyed a wider release than James Cameron's *Avatar* (2009) which, at its height, played in 3,461 theaters simultaneously" (Fallon 2019, 68). Brave New Films in fact surpassed Anne Phillips's goal of 2020 screenings between September 2019 and November 2020. If we estimate thirty people per screening, which would be conservative, that would add up to 60,600 viewers, almost certainly more than a theatrical release would have garnered, given that people do not want to pay, as Greenwald said, to watch "films on difficult subjects."

Live screenings in noncommercial contexts have many other virtues as well. They bring together a number of different mechanisms for generating "political agency." The film itself is powerful, and in the best cases it is shown on a large screen with high-quality equipment so that the sheer visual and auditory impact is enhanced. In the next chapter I will focus on the film itself and its power to move people emotionally. Here I continue to draw out the ways that the film, in this case via the group screening, works as part of the networked infrastructure of a potential social movement.

One part of that has to do with the bodily physicality of the screenings. Both film and social media create "publics," but publics in this sense are still, as we say, virtual. Screenings bring some part of those publics into real bodies in real time, and those occasions in turn lend a certain sense of reality to, and personal involvement in, those publics. Networks are a little more personal/physical, made up of many face-to-face persons and groups. They are also activated through personal, one-to-one contacts of the sort done by Anne Phillips and the Outreach team. Still, they are abstract entities, and the screening with a physical audience vivifies them, en-livens them, real-izes them in real time with real social others.

Another major part of the movement power of screenings emphasizes not just the physical coming together but the socialness of the event, the fact that the screening—unlike a movie showing in a commercial theater—is specifically geared toward enhancing social interaction and the exchange of ideas, thoughts, feelings. The socialness often includes a reception or even a meal (in the case of one church screening I attended) before the film, and always a discussion time afterward. Here we are reminded of the arguments about the power of the combination of provocative texts and "association"—discussions of the news in coffeehouses in early modern Europe, discussions of the Bible in BECs in modern Latin America—in which the text is never a thing in itself but always a basis for social engagement and consciousness-raising about the issues of the text/film.

Both the embodied aspect and the social aspect are often further enhanced by a panel of speakers. In many cases the panel includes people who were actually in the film, but sometimes it is simply people who have had related experiences and/or are part of related organizations. One screening organizer in New York spoke of the value of having a veteran who had served in Iraq present at a screening of *Uncovered: The War on Iraq*: "A lot of folks want to be able to speak to somebody who has actually been to the war" (Christensen 2009, 88). These individuals or panelists speak live from the point of view of the film itself. They bring it bodily into the room, as it were, and also facilitate/energize the discussion.

Finally, I want to call attention here to the organizing role of the person who generates the screening and then leads the discussion afterward. I have not seen this point emphasized in the literature, but I was struck by it ethnographically. The organizer might be an ordinary citizen who saw a trailer on her phone and decided to pull together a group of neighbors or friends for a screening in her living room. But most people who decide to host screenings are, in all likelihood, activists of one sort or another already. They tend to be people who are in charge of something—a community center leader, a teacher/professor/head of school, a minister, a politician, a staff member of an NGO, and so on. This person puts out the energy to organize the event, taking "organize" in the ordinary sense of arranging all the details—booking the space, setting up the projector, ordering the food, and such. But this person also operates as an organizer in the political sense. In this role they will invite allied groups to attend the event and set up "resource tables" full of relevant literature. They will also play an active (and in my experience always tactful) role in the discussion, guiding it in directions relevant to the film's issues, and cognizant of the goal of moving the participants toward some kind of action afterward.

I turn then to some ethnographic observations on screenings. Largely because they were scattered all over the United States, I was only able to attend a small number of them, but I found them extremely revealing—there is just nothing like the kind of knowledge and insight one gains from ethnographic immersion—and provide a brief overview here.[7]

Before *Suppressed* was released, I attended two screenings of other BNF films. The first was in a community center in an African American neighborhood in Pasadena, which was scheduled to show one or two of the films in the *Healing Trauma* series. This is a series of short films about an organization in Los Angeles that works with formerly incarcerated persons to help them get their lives back on track. There were about thirty people present, cookies were available in the lobby, and several organizations doing similar work to the one in the film had set up tables in the lobby with pamphlets about their programs. In this case, unfortunately, the organizer of the event was never able to get the projector to work, so the film was not actually shown. But the event featured a panel of people who either had appeared in the film or worked for a related organization, and the leader was able to get a good discussion going between the panel and the audience.

The second screening was in a church in Hawthorne, south of Los Angeles. The event was scheduled for noon on a Sunday, and when I arrived I found that some of the congregation members were serving a full lunch to a crowd of about fifty people. I was welcomed by the minister and urged to take part in the lunch.[8] Afterward some people peeled off, but about thirty of us repaired to the room where the projector was set up. Unfortunately, the minister couldn't get it to work, and we eventually moved into the church itself, losing another fifteen or so people along the way. They were scheduled to show some of the films in the *Following Their Lead: Youth in Action* series. By the time the minister finally got the projector going, however, there was only time for one four-minute video from the series, *Youth Rise Texas*, about high school students organizing a voter registration campaign among youth in minority communities in Texas.[9]

Beyond the problems with the projector, and the reduced amount of time, the Q&A afterward was somewhat hampered by the fact that a number of members of the congregation did not speak much English.

Yet in the end even this rather chaotic event, like the first one, seemed to produce some good outcomes. As I wrote in my notes at the time: "The woman sitting next to me, an older white woman, said that it was 'amazing that the film was so short and yet it packed so much information about the voting issue.' Then a young man [the son of one of the immigrants with little English] said that 'it's true that many of the kids [in minority/immigrant communities] don't vote. So it's good that these kids in the film are fired up'" (field notes, June 30, 2019).

The remainder of the screenings I attended were of *Suppressed*. I went to the premiere in Atlanta on September 24, 2019 (discussed in the next chapter), and to five screenings in the Los Angeles area. The first was the LA premiere, held in the AME (African Methodist Episcopal) Church in the old West Adams district (about a hundred people), followed over the next few months by events at a private school in Santa Monica (about two hundred people), a community theater in the West Adams district (eight people),[10] an auditorium/theater at the University of Southern California (USC; about fifty people), and a theater/club venue in Santa Monica (about two hundred people).

Most of these events were followed by some kind of panel, or a discussion led by some representative individual. The LA premiere at the AME Church had a panel that included the pastor of the church, J. Edgar Boyd; representatives of two different interfaith activist organizations; and a representative of a voter action group who worked in the Los Angeles County Registrar's Office.[11] The screening at USC had a panel of representatives of various relevant student organizations on campus. The event in the theater/club in Santa Monica featured the Hon. Anthony Daniels, minority leader of the Alabama House of Representatives, who acted as a kind of panel of one, taking questions about voter suppression and voter activation.[12] The event at the private school in Santa Monica did not include a panel, but Robert Greenwald himself was present and held a Q&A session.

In all cases the film produced an intense discussion about issues surrounding voting. The film's primary message—that voter suppression is widespread and strategically complex; that it is being intentionally pursued in order to suppress the votes of minorities, young people, the elderly, and other presumed Democratic voters; and that voter suppression is more devious and imaginatively underhanded than you could possibly imagine—that message came through loud and clear. At least one person at every screening expressed shock over the great extent, and strategic complexity, of voter suppression tactics. People who thought they already understood the problem well were particularly shocked at what they didn't know but learned from the film. The moderator at the event in the Santa Monica club said, "I knew all this but I was outraged!" (field notes, November 21, 2019). At the USC screening, one of the panelists said, "I've been doing research about voting rights. I thought I knew a lot. But this movie is over the top!" Another panelist said almost the same thing—"I knew a lot about voter suppression but this is crazy!" (field notes, February 13, 2020). And at the screening at the private school in Santa Monica, Greenwald himself said another version of the same thing: "He said that when he started this project he had no idea that voter suppression was this deep and wide and organized. He said the film gets people's hearts racing" (field notes, November 21, 2019).

Another major theme of the discussions was the relationship between voting issues and the African American community. The emphasis in the film is on the many ways in which the suppression is imposed on the community from the top down, by Republicans in positions of power seeking to win at any cost. But from the point of view of many in these mostly African American community audiences, there was also a problem at the grass roots, a problem of voter apathy in the African American community. Several speakers emphasized that there was extremely low voter turnout in that community. One of the speakers at the Los Angeles premiere said, "What you see in the film is happening here. We [African American citizens] have a responsibility to vote. The turnout is so low, the mayor [of Los Angeles] was elected with only 10% of eligible voters voting" (field notes, October 4, 2019). One of the speakers at the community theater in West Adams spoke of "the incredibly low voter turnout in her [African American] community, how Obama won the primary against Hillary Clinton with only a 7% turnout." She said, "It is very discouraging, people are not engaged, the problem is lack of civic engagement" (field notes, December 15, 2019). The Alabama state representative at the club in Santa Monica said, "Our efforts have to be about our [African American] sisters and brothers who don't vote, who think their vote doesn't count" (field notes, February 18, 2020). The film shows that voter suppression is directed against Black voters—but as the preceding comments highlight, the film focuses on Black *voters*, who would vote if they could, not the many alienated or otherwise detached people who don't try to vote in the first place. The issue is obviously complex, and the discussion format was able to enrich and intensify the film's message from the grassroots point of view.

Finally, there is the theme of the importance of getting active about the issue, which is of course the whole point of the film and the screening, and which was brought up in different ways at all of the events. At the premiere at the AME church, one of the panelists said in response to a comment from the audience, "Don't get depressed—organize! Get creative!" (field notes, October 4, 2019). At the community theater in West Adams, one of the panelists responded to a question by saying, "We have to take responsibility, be involved. There's a place for everybody [in community organizing]." The host of the event added, "Yes, just show up!" (field notes, December 15, 2019). At the screening at the private school in Santa Monica, an audience member asked, "What's the most impactful thing I can do?," which gave Greenwald the opportunity to make his pitch for people to get involved, whether by hosting more screenings, or finding an organization to work with, or letting others know about the film (field notes, November 21, 2019). At the same time, the discussions in all the venues about registering voters, turning out the vote, and motivating disaffected members of the African American community to get involved were themselves preludes to activism.

A Brief Note on "Preaching to the Choir"

It seems probable that the people who see BNF films, follow BNF on social media, or belong to organizations with which BNF partners are already predisposed to agree with the company's politics. This raises the question of how likely BNF films are to change people's minds and thus bring about significant shifts in political alignments, whether on particular issues or in general.

While it does seems likely that Brave New Films is for the most part "preaching to the choir," as it is often put, a few brief notes are in order. First, Greenwald has frequently expressed the hope that people can be persuaded by some points in the films even if they disagree with others.

For example, he said about *Iraq for Sale* that viewers might not agree with him about the war, but they might still be outraged by the profiteering. This strategy of highlighting *both* the moral *and* the material injustice is seen in many other BNF films as well, not only because it is important but also because it has that alternative persuasive potential.

Second, it seems that the screenings, as distinct from the social media lists and the partnering networks, have the capacity to reach more politically diverse audiences. This, in my limited observations, seemed to be true of the faith groups, where I could see at the screenings that the audiences/congregations were by no means politically homogeneous, and the Q&As came from a variety of positions. This might be true for student screenings as well, where many young people are relatively open and are still trying to figure out where they stand politically.[13]

Finally, it is worth emphasizing the difference between agreement and activation. Many people might agree with the political positions implicit or explicit in BNF films, but that does not mean they will do anything about the issues. The films are meant to inspire, incite, and get people to act on those issues. To do that, they do more than "preach," insofar as that metaphor suggests a kind of didactic reiteration of known ideas. As we have seen, they strive to provide surprising facts and to reveal hidden patterns, such that even people who thought they knew a lot about the issues were amazed, shocked, and thus perhaps more likely to act.

Activism as the Vision

I return here to the question of "vision." We saw that the Brave New Films vision statement was quite broad and open—"Our vision is an open democratic society that encourages rigorous debate, opportunity, and justice for all"—and suggested that we needed to look at their films to get a more specific sense of what they hope to bring about. For one thing, we could tie the terms of the statement to the content or subject matter of the films, as discussed in the previous chapter—the critiques of capitalism, racism, and incipient fascism—and argue that the vision behind the work of Brave New Films is of a society where those things are abolished. This is certainly true and should be underlined first.

At the same time, I want to make a slightly different point, to say that the most visionary moments of the films are not about the future, but about real moments of democratic action itself, in the here and now. These include both those classic images of activism, street demonstrations, and those less public images of communities in action, town meetings. Thus *Outfoxed* ends with a series of experts and activists saying some version of "You as citizens have power if you take it," showing demonstrators massing with signs in front of local media stations. *Suppressed* has a more elaborate version of this kind of ending. We see historic footage of the confrontation between the Black marchers and the police in Selma; we see people in the streets in the present day, marching and chanting. Somebody says at a rally, "We have the power to change this!," and the crowd erupts with cheers. Finally in this same vein, most of the videos in the series called *Following Their Lead: Youth in Action* also include footage of the excitement of collective demonstration—the crowds, the passion, the unity, the inspiring speeches.

Other BNF films show a different form of democratic participation, namely, community meetings where ordinary people debate and deliberate and express strong feelings over the futures of their communities. *Wal-Mart* ends with sequences in two different communities that collectively decide to keep Walmart out, with people excitedly cheering the outcomes, and further information about many similar community decisions scrolling up the screen. *Unconstitutional* uses the same strategy. In that film we learn about how the Patriot Act legislated many infringements of civil rights. The final sequence of the film shows a community meeting in which the participants vote unanimously to resist the act, declaring themselves a "Civil Liberties Safe Zone": people cheer wildly after the vote, and a scroll listing other communities that did the same thing rolls up the screen. In a phrase that has by now become somewhat hackneyed but that captures these events perfectly, this is what democracy looks like, not in some distant future but in real times and places in the present.[14]

Activist anthropologists David Graeber and Jeffrey Juris have both written about what they call "prefigurative politics," which involves not only opposing power and injustice in society at large but also, at the same time, creating a radically egalitarian social world within their activist groups that "prefigures" the world they hope to make in the future. Thus Graeber writes of the anarchists with whom he was involved as embracing a "genuine, living utopianism—the idea that radical alternatives are possible and that one can begin to create them in the present" (2009, x; see also Graeber 2002). And Juris writes of a particular action of his network that produced "the lived experience of prefigured utopian worlds" (2008, 156).

There are certainly differences between the politics of Brave New Films and those of the more radical, direct-action groups in which both Juris and Graeber were involved.[15] Yet I think it is not too much of a stretch to see the moments when ordinary Americans spontaneously take to the streets to protest racism, or organize massive transnational rallies against sexism, or convene town meetings to protest the subversion of democracy, as prefigurative in their own ways. This is so not only because they embody a kind of exhilarating collectivism, although that is an important point of connection with the exhilaration of direct action that we learn about in Juris's and Graeber's ethnographies. It is also because Brave New Films makes a point of showing us what Greenwald calls the victories, the ways collective action can in fact make a difference in the present and thus sustain a vision for a better future.

We still need to ask how, in practice, BNF tries to activate people specifically through their films. What is it within the films themselves—beyond showing the true state of the world—that might turn people to action? And what is it in the larger filmic experience—the screenings to which BNF is so committed—that might also create this effect? For this we turn to the next chapter.

4 Affective Agency

THE POWER OF THE FILM

In September 2019 I attended the world premiere of *Suppressed: The Fight to Vote* in Atlanta, Georgia. As sketched earlier, *Suppressed* is a critical examination of the rather astonishing array of mechanisms of voter suppression, and of the effects of voter suppression on the civic participation of minorities, especially African Americans, and other vulnerable voters. The specific case for the film is the 2018 Georgia gubernatorial election, in which Stacey Abrams, the former Democratic Leader of the House of the state of Georgia, ran against Republican Brian Kemp. Had she won, Abrams would have been the first Black woman to become a state governor. Kemp, for his part, was Georgia's secretary of state, which meant that he was in charge of elections; he continued to perform that role even after he became a candidate, which was the first of many irregularities, if not outright illegalities, in the process.

The film documents the extensive purging of the voter rolls before the election, and the closing of many polling places on various spurious grounds. We also hear from people who applied for absentee ballots but never received them. Thus many would-be voters were prevented from even coming to the polls. On Election Day itself, would-be voters encountered a variety of other barriers to voting, some related to arcane voter-ID issues, and others to an insufficient numbers of voting machines, even as we see shots of oversupplied and unused voting machines in wealthier/white precincts. We also see extremely long lines of people waiting to vote at many precincts, and we hear would-be voters talking of waiting two, three, or four hours in those lines. Many who did make it to the polls had to give up. In the end, Brian Kemp claimed victory with a margin of more than fifty thousand votes, about the number of people that experts estimate had been prevented from voting. Stacey Abrams refused to concede the election, though she "acknowledged" that Kemp would become the governor.

The film's premiere was held in the Auburn Avenue Research Library of African American Culture and History in Atlanta. There was a reception beforehand with a very nice buffet, and with Jim Miller, then executive director of Brave New Films, amiably pouring wine and bussing the buffet table. I chatted with various people at the reception, including a woman associated with the Library who said there weren't usually so many white folks at their events, and another woman who introduced herself as a retired teacher and, as it turned out, was also one of the interviewees in the film.

After the reception, we all went into the auditorium to view the film. The place was packed. Anne Phillips, BNF's director of outreach, had said earlier that the hall held more than 200 people but that she had had 350 RSVPs. Greenwald had said not to worry, that not everyone would show up. But it was literally standing room only.

There were some brief welcoming remarks by Anoa Changa, an Atlanta-based political analyst and attorney, representing the New Georgia Project, an organization for registering Georgia voters and one of BNF's launch partners for the film. Then the film was shown, with a good deal of audible reaction from the audience, mostly gasps at some of the more outrageous tactics of the Republicans, and at some of the more depressing statistics about the effectiveness of those tactics. When it ended, there was a standing ovation.

Following the film, speakers representing various activist organizations made brief comments about the work of their organizations, and there was a panel discussion involving a number of people who had appeared in the film. All of this together was, like all of BNF's films and activities, meant to get people politically active about the issues portrayed in the film.

In the present chapter I look closely at the event in terms of how it tries to accomplish this. I share with Brave New Films, and many theorists of social movements, the assumption that most people are not naturally inclined to "get involved." This issue is of particular import in the African American community, where, for understandable reasons, many people are alienated from the American nation-state and do not normally participate in its civic functions. In the following section, then, I look at this one film and its associated activity in terms of the production of what I am calling "affective agency," its strategies for engaging people emotionally and moving them to action.

A Note on Reception

It is a common practice in many forms of film studies to ask what kinds of subjectivity are being constructed for viewers by a particular film as a text, and that is what I will be doing with *Suppressed*. But I first need to make a brief excursion through the vexed question of audience "reception." It must immediately be granted that we do not know whether some or all viewers experience the film in the way to be argued here. The question of "reception" has always been a stumbling block for interpretive work of all kinds, including in anthropology, cultural studies, and film studies. We have perfected—I dare say—the arts of textual interpretation. We can see and show what is going on in a text with some precision, even if people might disagree about the interpretations. But we do not have good ways of discovering, with the same persuasiveness, what audiences are thinking or feeling in viewing the film. Quantitative studies of audience reception—questionnaires and surveys and statistical compilations—are easier to execute, but the nature of their data tends to be frustrating for those—like interpretive anthropologists—committed to a "thicker" understanding of the meaning and affect embedded in texts and (ideally) absorbed by viewers.

Qualitative, and specifically ethnographic, approaches to audience reception, on the other hand, seek to produce that kind of thickness, but they are hard to adapt to the study of ordinary movie audiences—that is, people who sit in a theater and watch a film and then leave (Hughes 2011). Anthropologists like Lila Abu-Lughod (2005) and Purnima Mankekar (1999) have had more success with television audiences, because they were able to join individuals/families watching television at home. Ethnographic sociologist Andrea Press has had good success with focus groups (1991), also mostly in relation to television programs. In these and other works, the ethnographer is able to discuss people's reactions with them at the time and thereby get a deeper sense of how they are responding to the film.

In my case I was fortunate that the industry for the kinds of films I have been interested in—independent (non-Hollywood) films in an earlier project (Ortner 2013b), and now political documentaries—routinely hosts screenings with audience Q&As afterward. By attending many such screenings, I have been able to gain some live, real-time access to audience responses. They tend to be somewhat scattered and unfocused, as people's questions and comments come from all different directions. But they do give us some clues as to what people are thinking and how they are reacting to the films in the immediate context of viewing. In addition, Brave New Films requests feedback from organizers of screenings, and I was able to access some of that material as well.

Affective Agency: Some Preliminary Notes

The question before us, then, is the construction of political subjectivity in films, and specifically what I am calling *affective agency*. I note first that I use *affect, emotions,* and *feelings* in more or less free variation, and in ordinary-usage, English-language ways. Within what has come to be called *affect theory*, there are important distinctions between affect, emotions, and feelings, and debates over those distinctions, but it would take us too far afield to discuss them here, and I will set this issue aside for a more specialized discussion.[1]

By *affective agency* I mean, in this context, the mobilization and shaping of strong feelings that incline people to take action to further social justice. Earlier I looked at the films in terms of how they develop critical understanding of the issues. Of course, critical understanding is itself infused with affect, so this is an artificial distinction. Nonetheless, in that context I wished to focus on the analytical and critical work of the films, and their specific ways of illuminating the problems of the world today. Here, on the other hand, I will focus on the emotional aspects of the film *Suppressed*, the ways it functions as a kind of consciousness-raising tool, designed to mobilize people through feeling and affect.

I draw on diverse sources for some basic theoretical framing. First, there is literature on the relationship between emotions and activism in general, before we look specifically at emotions and activism through film (Goodwin, Jasper, and Polletta 2001). An excellent example of such work is Deborah Gould's (2015) ethnographic study of the development of an activist sensibility among AIDS victims. Drawing on the work of anthropologist Clifford Geertz on the shaping of subjectivity, Gould shows that many AIDS victims began by feeling shame and reluctance to go public with their grievances, but were able to develop a more radical sensibility, and practice, in the course of engaging in activist politics (see also Kurik 2016, on "emerging subjectivity in protest").

Perhaps the most famous and inspirational work in this area is, once again, that of Paulo Freire. As discussed earlier, Freire developed the notion of *conscientização*, or "consciousness-raising," the pedagogical process through which oppressed people come to recognize the nature of their oppression and the necessity for radical/revolutionary action against it ([1970] 2000). In this context, Freire sometimes uses the phrase "just anger" or "just ire," which he opposes to "fatalistic docility" (2004, 59), and which he sees as one "indispensable starting point" of becoming an "active subject" of history (2004, 60–61). The role of anger in activist politics has also been taken up by philosopher Martha Nussbaum. Nussbaum sees (ordinary) anger as almost always involving an element of "payback," and she argues that, as such, it is detrimental to both interpersonal relations and effective social action. She discusses the writings of major leaders of social movements (Mohandas Gandhi, Martin Luther King Jr., and Nelson Mandela) and shows that they all renounce the use of anger in this sense. However, she makes a distinction between ordinary anger and what she calls "Transition-Anger," which is often "found when people get angry at a violation of an important principle, or at an unjust system" (2016, 36). Transition-Anger is defined as having no element of a wish for payback; instead, it is wholly oriented toward an active and constructive solution of the problem: "The *entire* content of one's emotion is, 'How outrageous! Something must be done about this'" (2016, 35).

Turning now to the specific question of the relationship between emotion and activism in film, one line of discussion emphasizes that much of the politically provocative power of the films is generated through the social processes of production and circulation discussed in the previous chapter. Here, by contrast, I will focus primarily on the film itself, and the ways it carries and provokes emotion specifically through its qualities as a film. But as already emphasized, Greenwald never relies wholly on the power of the film, so later in the chapter I will return to the screening experience and its emotional impact.

I begin with an article by Robert E. Terrill called "Mimesis and Miscarriage in *Unprecedented*" (2008), which discusses one of Greenwald's first activist films. Terrill looks at this film about the 2000 presidential election with the same question I am asking here: How does the film provoke social activism? He draws on Paula Rabinowitz's arguments to the effect that documentaries construct "subjects of agency" (1994), and Jane Gaines's arguments that they do so by way of what she called "political mimesis," providing viewers with models of political action, especially images of demonstrations and confrontations that convey a sense of the excitement of physical political participation in and of itself (1999).

Terrill expands Gaines's notion of political mimesis to include a wider range of audience responses: "The audience is encouraged not to ape the bodies on the screen but to assess possibilities of action and judgment . . . [and] to engage in inventive acts of their own" (2008, 137). By this criterion, however, Terrill finds that *Unprecedented* fails in its mission: the film "does not present a viable resource for political mimesis. It instead presents a Kafka-esque world in which effective moral action appears impossible. . . . The audience is left without ethical guidance: no one challenges power and prevails, no one emerges as a principled political actor, and no one models a viable way to behave" (2008, 137).

I find Terrill's point about this early Greenwald film close to the mark. It is interesting to compare *Unprecedented* and the more recent *Suppressed*, as both are concerned with the subversion of electoral democracy. And it is true that Greenwald offers viewers more possibilities for political mimesis in this extended sense in *Suppressed*, as we will see in this chapter. At the same time, I think that too much emphasis on the mimesis function fails to capture another way the film can work on the audience and provoke activist involvement, namely, by way of getting people angry at what they see on the screen. This has been emphasized by Jane Gaines in another article (2007), and it is certainly what emerged from my ethnography of audience reactions to *Suppressed*. While some people were clearly discouraged by the displays of power and immorality shown in the voter suppression tactics, most viewers were quite outraged and began to try to think of what actions they could take, very much in the manner of Martha Nussbaum's (clumsily phrased) "transition-anger." Moreover, both Gaines and Terrill put all the weight on the content within the boundaries of the film, while Greenwald hopes/assumes there will be a further step beyond the film, in which—more like the impoverished folks Freire was discussing—people will gather, express (strong) feelings, and discuss what they can do about their situation.

People and Their Stories

I will pursue the question of political affect in the film primarily through a focus on the people who are interviewed, whether as people who have been affected by the voter suppression tactics or as people who comment on the situation. There is no single term for the people in the film. Sometimes, with echoes of the commercial movie business, the people who appear in the film are collectively called "cast members," and the identification and recruitment of them is called "casting." In an impact report on another political documentary, they were called "on-screen subjects" (Borum Chattoo, Ramani, and Norwood 2020). Documentary film scholar Bill Nichols calls them "characters," and specifically "characters in direct address," meaning that they speak to an interviewer and through the interviewer to the audience (1981, 200). I will use a variety of terms and descriptive language throughout.

Characters in film in general are very important. They are central to the interpretation of narrative film, as important bodies of film theory are concerned with how the audience is drawn in through identification with, desire for, or antagonism to specific characters. Less attention has been paid to the role of people in documentary film, yet much of documentary relies heavily on real, named, identified persons; this is part of the reality function of this kind of film.[2] Nichols notes that documentaries that rely heavily on characters in direct address tend to be those "directed thematically toward questions of education, consciousness-raising, or radicalization" (1981, 202–3), which fits the case at hand nicely.

The staff at Brave New Films is very conscious of the importance of those real, identifiable people in the film: the would-be voters on the ground who tell their personal stories of suppression, and the experts and others who explain, comment on, or amplify the action. There is one clear "bad guy" in *Suppressed*: Brian Kemp. I will not have anything to say about him beyond pointing out that in two of his three appearances in the film, via clips from political ads, he is shown holding a lethal instrument, once a rifle and once a chainsaw. He is clearly the villain of the piece, but it is not Greenwald's intent to make voter suppression a matter of one bad individual, and Kemp does not play a major role in the film. There are also what might be thought of as "stars," well-known public figures like Stacey Abrams and Elijah Cummings, but structurally they play a kind of enhanced version of the role in the film of other experts/commentators and will be considered within that discussion.

I will begin with the people who tell the stories of their personal experiences. It became clear in talking to Greenwald and the staff at Brave New Films that these people are in a sense the bedrock of the films. At a screening of *Suppressed* at which outreach director Anne Phillips was present, one of the hosts asked her to comment on the film's power. She replied, "What works in the film is the personal stories, where you can hear from real people" (field notes, December 15, 2019). Likewise, when Greenwald was asked at a screening about the making of the film, he replied that a lot of the producers' work involves locating "the most compelling people with the most compelling stories" (field notes, December 15, 2019). And when asked in an interview about how his films reached both his political "base" and also viewers beyond that, Greenwald replied: "I think about this issue in terms of the message and the messengers. The messengers in *Wal-Mart* were Wal-Mart workers. They weren't people with partisan politics: they were people who worked there at all levels of the company. You can attack the film, you can attack me—that's all fine—but I don't think you can attack the *authenticity* of the people who were speaking. . . . I think that, at its core, it's a story about human beings, and I believe those human beings are the best ones to tell the story" (quoted in Haynes and Littler 2007, 28).[3]

These views about the importance of the people and their stories were echoed by several academic colleagues to whom I circulated the film for possible classroom use. In one case I asked a colleague what she found "most effective in the film." She replied, "People talking about their experiences. The struggles of people to vote. These were very moving, very powerful. That was what most stayed in [my] head. The experiences were incontestable, they just were what they were" (field notes, February 28, 2020). Another colleague showed the film to her class, and I asked for her feedback afterward. She wrote, "I feel like [the cast] created the impact of the film for me and my students. . . . The human dimension, and the creation of affect, was nearly wholly carried by the people—their range and diversity, THEIR feelings . . . , and their varied articulations of the same issues over and over" (email, March 26, 2021).

How does Brave New Films find the people for their films? *Suppressed* has fourteen people interviewed on camera in the role of expert (this includes professionals of various kinds but also figures like the pastor of a local church and a voter protection hotline volunteer) and nineteen people telling their personal stories of how they were in one way or another prevented from voting. I had a long interview with Laurie Ashbourne, the producer who did much of the work of finding and selecting the relevant people, which turns out to be a stunningly hard job—Greenwald described her at one screening as "working her ass off" to find people (field notes, November 21, 2019), and that is almost an understatement.

Finding the "experts" is a lot of work, but most of them have some kind of institutional base and/or public persona. It takes a lot of time, but it is doable, and because of space constraints I will not try to summarize that here. But how do you find the retired army sergeant or the cosmetologist or the twenty-something screenwriter who never received their absentee ballot, or whose polling location was closed, or whose voter registration paperwork was never processed? Here I list some of the kinds of sources and pathways Laurie used (all quotes from interview, February 14, 2020).

Some of it starts with a kind of ordinary search on Google: "Some involved just, you know, using Google with basic search terms: voter suppression or voting difficulties." Some of it starts with scouring the news about the events in question: "I would find a news story and find the reporter that was talking about it, and go to their Twitter feed. That hashtag, that Twitter feed, or the comments within that thread would then lead to something else, to something else, to something else." And again: "We scoured the Atlanta local news channels for people that they were talking to. So much of our B-roll, if you will, was news stories. That became sort of a character of its own." For example: "One of our cast members, the older man who's in the very beginning, Louis, was in a news story about the [earlier] 2016 election. His polling location was closed during the 2016 election. Somebody from the NAACP told his story and I just found it fascinating. We were like, 'Let's reach out and see if we can get a hold of him.' We reached out to the NAACP guy, who then reached out to him, because [Louis] doesn't have a computer or anything."

Some came from tracking through social media: "We relied on social media a lot because people would be filming themselves waiting in line, or filming their experience because they were so outraged."

Some came through relationships with organizations that were accumulating individual names and cases for their own reasons. Recall Jim Miller saying he contacted the lawyers at Fair Fight for names of people they were putting together for a legal case over voter suppression. Similarly, at the time of the interview with Laurie, she was already working on the next BNF film, about the impact of misdemeanors on the criminal justice system, and on people's lives: "We've been reaching out to public defenders' offices and finding their caseloads. A lot of the stuff that comes up in searches is the really high-profile cases that have been heavily covered, like Sandra Bland and Ferguson. Starting on that and then finding the people who are talking about it and the organizations that they belong to. Following that sort of rabbit trail; going on to Twitter, finding their Twitter feed, and seeing who's in their thread. It goes on and on and on."

The People of *Suppressed* I: Personal Stories

The people who tell their stories in the film are intentionally diverse in terms of age, gender, race/ethnicity, occupation, and so forth.[4] As noted earlier, Brave New Films has a strong commitment to diversity; more than half the staff are people of color. But there are specific reasons related to the film as well. For one thing, we learn at the very beginning of the film that the voter suppression strategy targets people of color. Although it does capture some white people, which allows those who operate the process to deny racist intent, it clearly has a disproportionate effect on Black communities and other communities of color. In addition, the filmmakers want to reach as wide an audience as possible and to provide ways for people of any age, gender, race, ethnicity, and so on to make a personal connection to the film. As Laurie put it, "We want to make sure we're representing all walks of life. [We want the viewer to feel,] 'This could happen to you. This is why you should care.'"

I thought about selecting a few of the characters to present here, but a good deal of the impact comes from the sheer number and variety of them, so I will—briefly—present them all. Each one tells a story of how they were in one way or another prevented from voting, and I will sketch the content and also try to capture some of the affect with which they are infused.

The first section of the film is called "Polling Places." Here we meet Louis Brooks, an eighty-nine-year-old African American retired mill worker. He says he remembers 1965 or '66, when Black people got the vote. He swore he'd never let anything stop him. He used to walk to a nearby polling place to vote, but they closed it in 2016. He knows that other polling places have been closed in majority-Black precincts as well, and says in a depressed tone, "Maybe they just don't want Black people to vote."

We next meet Linda Marshall, a sixty-five-year-old African American retired teacher and government worker. Marshall had recently moved to the state of Georgia. She tells us that she has always made a point of being registered and had sent in her voter registration paperwork as soon as she got to the state. But the paperwork was not processed, and she learned too late that she was not registered after all. She says sarcastically, "Welcome to Georgia."

The next section of the film is introduced by a placard that says "The Purge," and we hear from Stacey Hopkins, a young community organizer, who tells us in an angry but jokey way that she received "THE PURGE NO-TICE," which informed her that she had been purged from the registration rolls for reasons that had nothing to do with the reality of her situation. We also meet Jennifer Hill, a young white business owner who reads her purge notice out loud to the camera, similarly commenting sarcastically along the way about how none of the given reasons made any sense: she owns the same home she did before, she has paid her taxes, and so on.

The next section is called "Absentee Ballots." Here we meet Norman Broderick, a Black retired army MP. He talks about how he had always voted absentee while he was away on duty, in both Iraq and Afghanistan, and had never had a problem. Now he is back in the United States but is working out of state, so he requested an absentee ballot again, but it never came. He comments that it was easier to vote from Iraq than from South Carolina. He ends by saying, "It still pisses me off."

We also meet Peggy Xu, a young Asian American screenwriter who was living in DC and requested an absentee ballot, but it never came. She was clearly upset about this, and when she polled some friends online, she learned that this had happened to more than forty people in her network.

Finally we arrive at Election Day, when we encounter many more people who face even more roadblocks that keep them from voting. We first meet Erika Underwood-Jackson, a young African American woman who is filming herself and others waiting in line to vote. She talks about how slowly the line is moving: "We move a few steps and then we stop for a long time. And then we move a few steps again." The film will come back to her and her video several times as she chronicles the grindingly slow progress at the poll. She and others talk about waits of two or three or four hours, during which people who are unable to wait peel off. We will learn eventually that most of the majority-Black precincts had a very small number of voting machines, which was a major reason for the slowness, and one of the strategies for reducing the vote of these and other probable Democratic voters.

Another strategy of voter suppression involved provisional ballots. Here we meet Jocelyn Kimble, an African American cosmetologist who, after waiting in line for a long time, is told at one polling place that she is in the wrong place, and gets sent downtown where she finds another long line. Once again she is told she is in the wrong place and is told to go back to her original polling place. At that point, she needs to go home, but she had made a promise to an elderly lady who had emphasized how important it was to vote, so she goes back to the first polling place. She eventually votes with a provisional ballot, but it turns out that people who used provisional ballots needed to return three days later to verify their identity. Jocelyn learns later that her vote was never counted.

We next meet Connie Ogletree and Barbara Young, identified simply as residents of Fulton County. Barbara Young is a very elderly African American lady who is legally blind, and Connie Ogletree, her elderly companion, is helping her out. Barbara is told that her name does not appear on the rolls and is sent away.

Carlos Del Rio is a middle-aged Latino man, chair of the Global Health Department at Emory University. From Carlos we learn about the exact-match law in Georgia, which specifies that the name on the registration rolls must exactly match the name on the photo ID that the would-be voter presents. The people at the polling place try to turn Carlos away because the name on his voter registration is "Del Rio" with a space, while the name on his driver's license is "DelRio" without a space and thus violates the exact-match law. Carlos argues with them, and in this case he wins and succeeds in voting, possibly because of his very professional appearance, but he is still angry about the episode.

Then we meet a series of seven students from the various local universities, almost all of them Black or Latinx. All of them are turned away on various spurious grounds of ineligibility, including Phoebe Einzig-Roth, who is told that she does not appear to be a citizen. She is dumbfounded, as she had been born in New York City and had brought a slew of identification items with her, which the poll workers refused to look at. Phoebe tells us, still more or less in shock, that she had been learning about voter suppression in her history class just that morning, and now it was happening to her in 2018.

These are the ordinary people telling their various personal stories of having tried to vote and having been blocked by a whole array of different tactics. We can see and almost hear the affect infusing these stories. People are some combination of frustrated and angry, although the anger is expressed in different individual ways—through actual statements of anger, as when Norman Broderick says, "I'm still pissed off"; through annoyed or aggravated tones of voice; through a certain kind of sarcastic or ironic humor; and through a kind of sorrowful resignation that in effect says, "This is what's going on and we can't seem to do anything about it."

We can see this as the first moment of the (sought-after) formation of the viewer's political subjectivity. The viewer is invited to identify with these folks and their experiences, which should not be difficult, as most people watching the film will have had frustrating and anger-making experiences with some kind of bureaucratic red tape, stonewalling, and runarounds. The viewer is also invited to feel a sense of caring about these folks, whether because they are frail and elderly, or because they are young and idealistic, or simply because they are ordinary citizens who have tried to do the right thing and have been screwed (I can't think of a better word) by the system. Both the identification and the caring draw the viewer emotionally into the film, and into the various forms of affect the people express.

Because these characters are individuals telling us about their individual experiences, we cannot learn from this level of the film about the wider ramifications of the voter suppression. That level of the story is carried in part by information presented on the screen, in the form of text panels, graphics, and statistics. But it is also carried by the experts and commentators, who put the individual stories in wider perspective and infuse them with an additional layer of affect, as we see next.

The People of *Suppressed* II: The Experts and Commentators

The people who comment on the issues of the film, as opposed to the people who tell their personal stories, represent various kinds of expertise. Some are academics who have conducted research on the subject. Some are practitioners in the field at issue, including lawyers and others who work in organizations dedicated to the protection of civil rights in general, and/or voting rights in particular. And some are members of the community who have some kind of position of expertise/authority, including community organizers, clergy, and so on.

Many documentary filmmakers resist having experts and commentators in their films, arguing that it is too didactic, that it represents too much schooling of the audience, that it makes documentaries boring, and so on. Greenwald has no such qualms: he relies heavily on experts and commentators to help us understand the issues. I would note in advance, however, that they tend to be people who are closely involved in those issues, and often very committed to them. They explain things not from on high, as the term *expert* might suggest, but from the perspective of an engaged and often locally grounded expertise. They thus contribute to the mix not only information and clarification but also another dimension of the film's affective quality.

The film begins with comments from Carol Anderson, professor of history, chair of African American Studies at Emory University, and author of *One Person, No Vote: How Voter Suppression Is Destroying Our Democracy* (2019). Anderson sets the tone by saying, "Pull back that veneer, and you see something really rotten happening. It's almost like termites, coming in. They're in the wood. They're eating the wood away. You don't even realize your house is getting ready to collapse until it's almost too late." Anderson appears periodically throughout the film, commenting on various aspects of the voter suppression process and its impact on the African American community.

We next hear from Rashad Robinson, president of the activist organization Color of Change, who explains the implications of the 2013 modifications of the 1965 Voting Rights Act. These modifications allowed states much more leeway in their management of elections and thus opened the door to many of the questionable, possibly illegal, and often outrageous practices of voter manipulation that we see in the film.

Carol Anderson then comes back and says emphatically that the process of voter suppression is "very bureaucratic, very mundane, very routine; but it is *lethal*."

The next section of the film is called "Polling Places." This is where we heard eighty-nine-year-old Louis Brooks talking about how the election authorities had closed his nearby polling place. In this section we meet a number of different experts: Bobby Jenkins, a retired school superintendent for Randolph County; Loretta Brown, state adviser for the Georgia NAACP youth and college division; and Sean Young, the legal director of the ACLU of Georgia, all of whom comment on the ways the closure of polling places creates hardships for various categories of voters—the Black, the poor, the elderly—and thus suppresses their votes.

In the next section, called "Registration," we meet Nse Ufot, executive director of the New Georgia Project, dedicated primarily to registering voters. It was in this section that we heard Linda Marshall talk about how she had recently moved to Georgia and attempted to register to vote, but that her application was never processed. Ufot explains the irregularities of Brian Kemp's role, serving simultaneously as both secretary of state and candidate for election; she also explains how Kemp was legally able to hold back many applications for voter registration, like Linda Marshall's, and thus keep them out of the voting pool.

In the next section, "Purge," we had met Stacey Hopkins, who ranted sarcastically about having received "THE PURGE NOTICE," and Jennifer Hill who read her purge notice to the camera in disbelief. Here we meet expert Vanita Gupta, president and CEO of the Leadership Conference on Civil and Human Rights, who comments that many of the purged voters, like the ones we just saw, were actually eligible and were unlawfully removed.

In the next section, "Absentee Ballots," we had met Norman Broderick, the retired army MP, and Peggy Xu, the young screenwriter, both of whom had requested absentee ballots but did not receive them. Here the expert is Lauren Groh-Wargo, who had been Stacey Abrams's campaign manager and is now the chief executive of Fair Fight Action, the voting rights NGO created by Abrams in the wake of the 2018 election fiasco. We hear an off-screen voice, apparently that of a newscaster, say that the election is now a "dead heat" because there are so many absentee ballots. Groh-Wargo says, with evident satisfaction, "We caught them off guard by running such a large-scale program. We mailed 1.6 million African Americans an absentee ballot application."

Then we arrive at the long final section, "Election Day," where we have seen the endlessly long lines at the polls in mostly Black precincts, and where we have heard the stories of the bad experiences of Erika Underwood-Jackson, Jocelyn Kimble, Barbara Young, Carlos Del Rio, and multiple students, who waited in those long lines, and/or were turned away on spurious grounds, and/or were given "provisional ballots" that were never counted, and so forth. The shots of long lines in the mostly Black precincts are contrasted with shots from the white/wealthier precincts, where we see banks of unused voting machines. The experts in this context include Rich DeMillo, chair of computer science at Georgia Institute of Technology, who notes, "If you have a fixed resource [like voting machines], an easy way to suppress the vote is to just make that resource unavailable to the people who you don't want to vote."

Commenting on the impact of the long lines, Carol Anderson returns and says emphatically, "Long lines reduce voter participation. The research on this is crystal clear." The Reverend Billy M. Honor, pastor of Pulse Church, Fulton County, adds, "All it takes is a little walking away in 159 counties, a little here, a little there, and you influence an election." Finally, after a few earlier glimpses of Stacey Abrams in news clips, she comes directly on-screen in the film and comments on all the problems on Election Day: "I have been with these folks in their homes, in their living rooms. I know them. To see them subject to these conditions—it just broke my heart."

There is one more section, titled "Provisional Ballots," but perhaps we have learned enough to say a few more general things about the experts and commentators. As noted earlier, partly they play a role of explaining and clarifying things in the film that might not be clear or obvious to the viewer. Yet in virtually every case they explain things not only in terms of the mechanics (e.g., about how the provisional ballots work) but also in terms of their unequal effects on the voting population. They take the personal stories up to a broader level, where we are shown that this was not simply a fluke visited upon particular individuals; rather, it was a systematic pattern of manipulation that had systematic effects on outcomes for particular groups—students, the elderly, and especially African Americans—all of whom tend to vote disproportionately in favor of Democratic candidates.

The experts/commentators thus both broaden and amplify the political implications of the personal stories. They also, at least in some cases, amplify the affect. For example, in the statement quoted above, Stacey Abrams amplifies the sense of caring that we might feel, in sympathy with all the people who are being manipulated, when she says "it broke my heart." Some of the other commentators amplify the anger we heard from some of the people telling personal stories: for example, Nse Ufot comments with a hard face on Brian Kemp's double role in the election: "You have an umpire who is also playing in the game."

The amplification of anger is particularly clear in the role played by Carol Anderson throughout the film. Anderson looks and sounds angry from the very beginning, when she gives the analogy of the termites eating the woodwork. She reappears throughout the film, sometimes on-screen and sometimes speaking over a visual sequence, and she sounds angry throughout. In the "Purge" sequence, for example, we hear her sarcastically enumerating the spurious reasons a voter can be purged: "If you haven't voted in the last few elections, they'll PURGE you! . . . If you move within the same county, they'll PURGE you! . . . If you don't return a postcard from the secretary of state, they'll PURGE you!"

We may recall here the earlier discussion of what Paulo Freire called "just ire" (2004, 59), anger about injustice in the social/political/economic world, expressed not only on behalf of the self but on behalf of all those upon whom it is visited. Virtually any expression of anger at any point in the film is of this nature; it is then in a sense gathered up and shaped into the powerful speech that Stacey Abrams gave at the end of the election and that is replayed in the film. Abrams "acknowledges" that

Brian Kemp will be sworn in as governor of the state of Georgia. But, she says, with a frowning face, in a loud voice, in a rhythmic pattern while chopping the air with her hand, "This. is. not. a. speech. of. concession! Because concession means to acknowledge an action is right. true. or proper! As a woman of conscience and faith, I cannot concede that!"

And I would suggest that there is one more level of impact of the experts. While "explaining" is their most visible role in the film, one could also see them as inspiring, as people who have made lives and careers in social justice, whether as clergy, or in social justice NGOs, or in electoral politics, where they continue to fight against all the ugly things we have seen in the film. I emphasized in the last section how the viewer is invited to identify with the people who tell their stories of having been "suppressed." But the experts and commentators may also serve as points of identification, whether for middle-class and/or educated viewers who recognize themselves in those positions, or for young people of all backgrounds who aspire to play similar roles themselves someday. It is also relevant to note here that many, perhaps even a majority, of the experts in *Suppressed* and some other recent BNF films have been women and persons of color; Greenwald calls this "one of our most important contributions" (email, February 28, 2021).

Thus far I have interpreted the film in terms of the responses it arguably seeks to provoke. This is a standard and potentially powerful mode of film interpretation, but as many critics have pointed out, it tells us nothing about the responses of real people in real time and space. Viewer reception is not a central issue in many kinds of film studies scholarship, but it is a very important question for the anthropology of film in general, and for the relationship between film and social movements in particular. Fortunately, because of Brave New Films' outreach system, we are able to learn what at least some viewers have actually thought and felt on viewing the films. I look at some of this material here, specifically with respect to the question of affect.

Affective Reception

When a BNF film is shown at an organized screening, the outreach director follows up by emailing a brief questionnaire. The first question is, "Did you complete your screening of [in this case] *Suppressed: The Fight to*

Vote?" If yes, the next item is, "Great! We'd love to hear how it went. Please include any reactions or anecdotes from your screening." In other words, the request for feedback is quite open-ended.

I present here a sample of replies, most of them from screenings by organizations involved in some aspect of civil rights and/or voting rights.[5] Some of the replies were simply descriptive, along the lines of "We showed the film, had a good discussion afterward, and will recommend it to other organizations." But many, perhaps the majority, described some kind of emotional impact from the screening.

There was first of all something like shock in learning of the scope of the problem: "The Racial Justice Committee of our . . . chapter saw this last night and were beyond astounded at what the Republicans and the Brian Kemp campaign did to steal the gubernatorial victory from Democrat Stacey Abrams." And: "Everyone who watched the documentary were just appalled at the blatant rigging of the 2018 election." And: "I was involved in voter registration efforts in the Augusta, Georgia, area extensively last year with the [organization]. So, I was aware of a lot of the issues discussed in the film. However, the film still blew my mind at the sheer magnitude of the voter suppression."

Another group used a language of being strongly "moved": "Our audience of about 75 was *so moved by this film*. In the whole room not a sound was heard throughout the entire 35-minute screening—there was that kind of *intense* listening going on. After the film, people were visibly upset and yet, determined to take action" (all emphases in the original). And: "Everyone was moved. We had a natural conversation afterward. Most everyone in the room had no idea that polling sites were closing, how purges happened, and that Kemp had the power he did to manage the election alongside running in the race. People were moved and upset."

This mode of being "moved" was often tied to the personal stories, and included compassion for the people who were affected: "The film was very well received—many of us were in tears by the end of the movie. We loved the amount of diverse examples of voter suppression that were featured [in the personal stories]. The evidence is overwhelming." And: "Everyone was personally moved. It was disheartening to hear their personal stories. Everyone said how hurt they felt for these people denied their right to vote. . . . Perhaps the most moving stories were of the woman who repeatedly was told the wrong information, and of the veteran. Overall it was very emotional."

Finally, some of the responses emphasized anger. For example: "Viewers noted that this film was a roller coaster of emotions from anger at the systems of oppression to the hope of ultimately overcoming." And: "People were angry and said that shit like THIS is why we had to continue our fight to see that this administration is removed." And: "The following reactions were unanimous. (1) Extreme anger over what took place and without any repercussions. (2) We must do everything we can to get this viewed by other organizations we belong to." It should be noted that all of these comments expressing anger are followed directly by some statement of a call to action. They say not only "How outrageous!" but also "Something must be done about this!" (see Nussbaum 2016, 35).

Yet the filmic event contains even further strategies for arousing what I am calling affective agency, to which we now turn.

The Narrative Arc

Suppressed, like most other BNF films, has a very systematically articulated structure. There are, as we have already seen, sections or "chapters" with headings: "Polling Places," "Purge," and so on. Within each chapter, in turn, there is a clear progression: one or two people tell their personal stories, one or two experts comment on some of the broader implications of those stories, and finally the film displays statistics to spell out the broadest implications of the issue. At the end of the chapter on the closure of polling places, for example, we see this text: "Since 2012 Georgia has closed 214 polling places, affecting almost 1.3 million voters. 75% of them were in majority African American counties."

This progression is central to one of Greenwald's strategies of affectively engaging the viewer, starting with the personal stories, and then moving the viewer to a more abstract or intellectual grasp of the issues. Describing a "theory that guides our work," he wrote, "First get the heart, then the head will follow" (email, February 28, 2021; see also Haynes and Littler 2007, 29). Put in these terms, the educational and critical function of the films are seen as the end point of one progression of the film's logic.

Again, though, Greenwald does not simply want to educate people; he wants to move them to action. Although every element of the film is meant to contribute to that process, it is especially visible in the overall arc of the story, and peaks at its end. As we have just seen, most of the film is taken up with stories and comments and visuals that carry sustained negative affect—frustration, resignation, irritation, anger, outrage. But like any political organizer, Greenwald recognizes that one cannot leave viewers in that negative, "disheartened" condition: they must be made to feel that political action can be effective, and they must be inspired and energized to get up and do it. I overheard this exchange during the editing of the final section of the film, as Greenwald looked over the shoulder of producer Casey Cooper Johnson. Casey was not happy with the final segment and said, "I don't feel the victories." Greenwald was clearly unhappy too and said, "It's *so important*. People will have been seeing all this negative stuff and we *must, must* show people that there are victories'" (field notes, July 19, 2019; emphasis in the original).

The final section of the film can thus be seen as redirecting and remolding all of the negative emotions into forms of political activism and agency. The film has, as they say in theater, a "big ending." "America the Beautiful" sung by Leslie Odom Jr. surges up on the soundtrack, and we see old black-and-white footage from the 1965 march on Selma, Alabama. We hear the Reverend Al Sharpton on the soundtrack exclaiming, "We are not going to let them take from us what our grandparents and parents fought and suffered and died for!" A little later we see and hear Representative Elijah Cummings say almost the same thing: "One year ago today, on my mother's dying bed, ninety-two years old, former sharecropper, her last words were, 'Do not let them take our vote away from us!'"

We also hear about whatever political victories can be counted at that point in time. Historian Carol Anderson makes a final appearance to tell us about a number of states that have proposed or even passed laws protecting voting rights; graphics light up the states in question on a map of the United States. We see clips of demonstrators in those states either demonstrating loudly in favor of the proposed legislation or happily cheering its successful passage. At the very end we see and hear a huge sea of demonstrators massed together and cheering, representing not a particular victory but the power of mass activation as such. And we see the final panel, which is also the tagline of the film: "If your vote didn't matter, they wouldn't be trying to stop it."

This finale is very important in terms of dramatizing the transformation of the negative energy of the film into the positive energy of political action. Many people will see the film online, and that is the last thing they will see. But from the point of view of Brave New Films, the ending is not necessarily the end, and there is yet one more step.

The Film Comes Alive

As we know by now, all BNF films are ideally viewed in the context of a live screening, with a local host serving as coordinator, and with discussion afterward. At some of these screenings, Greenwald himself and/ or a BNF staff member might participate in some way, or someone who appears in the film might attend and take questions. In the most fully developed events, a panel of several people from the film might be there to participate in a Q&A session. All of these live appearances serve to mediate between the experience of watching a nonliving object, a screen, and the living social world in which, hopefully, political action will take shape. At the premiere of *Suppressed* in Atlanta, Robert Greenwald was the first person to come out on the stage after the film, and he made this point explicitly: "This is the transitional moment when the film is turned over to all of you."

In my experience with live documentary screenings, both in the earlier independent film project and in this one, documentary filmmakers often make an effort to have some people from the film appear live afterward (Ortner 2013b, chap. 8).[6] In part this is related to the truth or reality function of documentary—the filmmaker says, in effect, "I didn't make this up. Here is the real person you just saw on the screen, and they will testify to its truth." But it is also clearly meant, and staged, to have a dramatic impact. The live appearance of the people from the film is never announced in advance. The people come out in the dark at the end of the film, before the lights come up, and take their seats on the stage. Then the lights come up, and there you see some of the heroes of the film in the flesh, and my sense is that audiences find this thrilling, almost magical, as if the people had stepped out of the screen and onto the stage. There is often a standing ovation at this point. This then is not only part of the film's truth-work, but part of its affective work as well.

Here I will discuss briefly the panel and other live action that took place on the stage after the premiere of *Suppressed* in Atlanta, in terms of both the intensification of the feelings already encountered in the film and the redirection of those feelings toward political activism. The moderator for the panel was Cliff Albright, a cofounder of the Black Voters Matter Fund, who also hosts a weekly radio show in Atlanta. The panel consisted of five people who appear in the film: Professor Carol Anderson and four of the folks who told their personal stories of suppression. Albright makes a few opening remarks and then asks each of the panelists to comment on their experience watching the film. With this question, he transforms the panelists from participants in the action of the film to audience members, like everyone in the room, who have just watched and reacted to the film. They create what almost feels like a current between the audience and the film.

Most of them begin by telling us that the strong feelings they felt at the time of the filming were reawakened by watching the film. Albright himself begins with an emotional comment, saying that he found himself "tearing up" while watching the film. Carol Anderson says, "I'm in a perpetual state of pissedness." She goes on, "I'm a historian, I know how hard people have fought for these rights, and then to watch this happen all over again—well, I'm just in this perpetual state." Norman Broderick, the retired MP, says he was "overwhelmed" by the film. Erika Underwood-Jackson, the young woman who filmed herself and the hundreds of other people waiting endlessly in line at the polls, said sorrowfully, "So many first-time voters were registered, and then were discouraged." And Phoebe Einzig-Roth, the New York–born American student who was told she was apparently not a citizen, repeated the sense of shocked awakening she felt at the time: "History is everything. You see it in your textbooks, and then it happens to you, and then it's not history anymore."

In addition, several of the panelists say something about turning those strong feelings into action. Linda Marshall, the woman who tried to register but whose paperwork was never processed, says, "We are at war. . . . They [the Republicans] are playing a long game. We have to play a long game too." Carol Anderson says, "It's all to discourage people. It's not just the one individual whose vote is suppressed, but everyone around them. *But Americans are fighters.*" And Norman Broderick tells us that his wife is a lawyer and that she said, "You can't just sit and fester, you have to DO SOMETHING."

The theme of "doing something" is picked up and amplified after the panel. Greenwald comes out again and urges the audience to sign up to host screenings. Then Lauren Groh-Wargo, the CEO of Fair Fight Action, comes out and speaks with extraordinary dynamism and passion. She talks about the various initiatives undertaken by Fair Fight Action to challenge the voter suppression movement and concludes, "We're going to win those challenges! We can do this! We have the knowledge and the power!"

We turn now to the final chapter and ask what are in effect the ultimate questions for any activist documentary: Did it work? Did it have some recognizable impact? Like the problem of "truth," the problem of "impact" is itself much debated in the documentary world: Should we even be asking that question? I will explore both the debate and some outcomes.

5 The Impact Question, and Conclusions

I began this book with a brief sketch of the role of "powerful texts" in some historic social movements. A central part of that role was the assumption by contemporary readers that such texts carried important truths. Another was the way such texts were read in social groups, where they generated discussion, debate, excitement. From the beginning, Brave New Films was committed to making and using their films in this way, and I have set the company within this tradition.

Brave New Films in turn was part of the rather spectacular takeoff of documentary film, and especially political documentary, starting in the first decades of the twenty-first century. (As noted earlier, by "political" throughout this book I have meant "on the left" unless otherwise indicated.) This was seen as a response in part to a series of real-world political crises at the beginning of the century, starting with the controversial presidential election of 2000, followed by the attack on the World Trade Center in 2001, Bush's invasion of Iraq in 2003, and so on. It was also seen as a response to the deterioration of the mediascape in the United States, including both the rise of right-wing media and mainstream media's abrogation of its responsibilities of fact-finding and of holding those in power to account.

Documentary has always been founded on a commitment to truthfulness; that has been central to its identity from the beginning. But this commitment was not always tied to a politically critical stance, and there are ongoing debates over whether it should be. Nonetheless, what has been distinctive about the surge of documentary in this era has been the degree to which it has taken up a much more critical and politicized position vis-à-vis the events of the world. Not all documentary today is "political," but it is safe to say that the political documentary is now much more central to the documentary scene than it was in the recent past.[1]

Brave New Films played a major role in that development. The company came on the scene early and fast, with some of the first critical films on the 2000 election, the invasion of Iraq, the rise of right-wing media, and more. Robert Greenwald also kept up an incredible pace of production: he made six (directed four, executive-produced two) full-length documentaries between 2002 and 2006. After that he slightly slowed the pace of the full-length filmmaking but went heavily into political videos on social media, creating as many as thirty-five short videos in a given year.

In framing what BNF does and how they go about doing it, I have used the concept of political agency, the idea of awakening in people an awareness of injustice and a desire to act against it. With affinities to Paulo Freire's *conscientização* and feminist "consciousness-raising," the idea of generating "agency," as both a desire to act and a sense of capacity to act, has been taken up in the literature on documentary film as a way of seeing the lived effects of this particular medium. The chapters of this book, in turn, have represented various inflections on the idea of political agency. In chapter 2, titled "Critical Agency," I looked at the corpus of BNF films in terms of the kinds of critical understanding of social issues the films seek to provide, and in terms of the "hegemonized ignorance" they seek to disrupt. In chapter 3, titled "Networked Agency," I looked at the ways in which the films are circulated socially, becoming parts of political networks and objects of social gathering and debate. In chapter 4, titled "Affective Agency," I looked at the ways in which the films seek to touch people emotionally, linking critical understanding with anger and other forms of affect that can move people to act.

The question that remains for these conclusions is what makers of political documentaries call "impact," of whether and how they, and we, can say that the films in some way "made a difference" in pushing back against power, violence, inequality, and injustice, and pushing forward the values of the good: peace, equality, cooperation, and justice.

Impact

"Impact" turns out to be a more complicated question than it might appear at first glance, starting with how to pose the question in the first place. Writing about the massive protests against the invasion of Iraq in 2003, and knowing that George W. Bush went ahead with the invasion anyway, sociologist David S. Meyer writes, "Did any of [those protests] change anything? Could they have? How? And how would we know if they did?" (2015, 386). He goes on to say, "The ways that movements make a difference are complex [and] veiled," may take unexpected forms, and may take a long time to appear (2015, 387).

The question of the social impact of film has grown to be an enormous industry. This includes something called "impact producers," individuals who will work with a filmmaker to enhance the impact of his or her film (Curtis 2015). A recent immersive webinar by DocNYC Pro, a major organization of and for documentary filmmakers, was called *Social Impact When the World Is Inside* (2020). It featured four different kinds of impact producers: one who helped individual filmmakers create more impact for their films; one who partnered with local activist groups to help them make their own films; one who basically functioned as a distributor for socially relevant films; and one who was part of an organization that focused on funding issues for independent filmmakers.

In addition, there are impact research organizations that develop strategies for measuring and evaluating the impact of particular films on individuals, and that generate detailed reports filmmakers can provide to donors, granting agencies, and boards of directors.[2] For example, Participant Media, a for-profit company that backs and finances socially conscious films for the commercial market, commissioned the Media Impact Project at the University of Southern California to conduct social impact studies on several of its films (*Food, Inc.* [2009], *Waiting for "Superman"* [2010], and *Contagion* [2011]). These studies were based on online survey research that asked individuals about their reactions to the films and about their likelihood of taking some kind of social or political or otherwise remedial action in relation to the films' issues. Similarly, the Center for Media and Social Impact at American University conducted an impact study for a documentary called *Milwaukee 53206* (2016). In this case the sponsoring organization held screenings similar to those sponsored by

Brave New Films, and the surveys were administered via people's smartphones at the screenings. Again people were asked about their experience of the film and about their likelihood of taking action afterward.

The findings of these studies are expressed in the form of statistics about individual opinions and individual behavior. From the impact report on *Food, Inc.*, for example, we learn that 84 percent of respondents checked "It changed my life!" and 80 percent answered yes to the question "After watching the film, do you feel like you could be a part of a social movement to reform agribusiness?" (Blakley et al., n.d.).[3] Yet the idea that films should have metrically measurable impact is highly contested, both by many filmmakers and by critics and observers who simply argue for taking a broader view of how films are supposed to work for their audiences (Fields 2014). Objections are directed against all the measurement and quantification, which reduces complex personal reactions to simple numerical answers. Objections are also directed against the idea that a film is effective primarily if it had some quantifiable behavioral effect—for example, if someone signed a petition after seeing the film. Bill Nichols, probably the leading authority on documentary film, echoes many others who argue that the primary function/effect of great documentaries is not to provide some direct pathway to political action but to transform the way we see the world. As he famously put it, "To see anew is to shift perceptual frames. To be moved to do so by works possessed of aesthetic power yields real but not necessarily quantifiable results" (2016a, 227).

I share the view that the "aesthetic power" of film is often deep and slow-acting in terms of lingering within and/or shaping subjectivity. Many of us have had experiences of particular films that we saw as young people that stayed with us for a lifetime.[4] This slow-acting depth is something that cannot be captured in the kinds of impact studies just noted; it requires the fine-grained understanding gained through ethnographic and interpretive approaches. But the objectives of activist filmmakers are different: they want to make an impact on the real world, and they want to make it *now*. They do not deny the point of aesthetic power—indeed, they affirm it strongly—but they do not see it as an end in itself. Rather, they seek to harness it for political purposes.

I join these filmmakers in not seeing social and political impact as being at odds with the aesthetic and affective workings of a film. Impact does, however, take a variety of forms, and it will be useful to sort some of these out. Before getting to the question with respect to BNF films, however, I want to look briefly at two interesting examples of what I take to be significant political impact. Both of these avoid the problems that comes with the survey research model.[5]

The first comes out of an academic study of the impact of the film *Gasland* (2010). *Gasland* is about the harmful effects of "fracking," the injection of chemicals into the ground in order to release and capture natural gas for commercial sale. The film won the Sundance Special Jury Prize of 2010, among other awards, and was nominated for an Academy Award in 2011.[6] The filmmaker, Josh Fox, had a clear political agenda: to use the film to try to stop this practice. He used a screening model similar to Brave New Films, in which community groups of various kinds hosted screenings with discussion and Q&As afterward.

The study was conducted by a group of sociologists and media studies scholars (Vasi et al. 2015) for scholarly purposes and not commissioned by people connected with the film. Taking as their unit of study cities that had held group screenings of the film, the researchers asked whether those cities were more likely to have shown some recognizable form of resistance against the inroads of the fracking corporations. The short answer, buttressed by a lot of technical methodology affirming the reliability of the results, is that yes, they were able to show that cities that had had group screenings of *Gasland* were (a) more likely to have mobilization of efforts to block the fracking and, beyond that, (b) more likely to actually pass legislation either blocking the practice completely or at least putting in place a moratorium pending further inquiry.

A second example concerns the film *The Invisible War* (2012), directed by Kirby Dick, about rape in the military. Dick provides overwhelming evidence in the film of how widespread the practice is, and of its terrible toll on the women (and some men) who are its victims. He was also able to gain access to some high-level officials in Washington to make a case for administrative and/or legislative action on this problem. Angela Aguayo summarizes the film's impact on policy and legislation, and I will quote her in full:

> In his 2014 memoir, *Worthy Fights*, Secretary of Defense Leon Panetta stated that watching *The Invisible War* was one of the main factors that influenced him to issue a directive ordering all sexual assault cases to be

handled by senior officers, ending the practice of commanders adjudicating the cases from within their own units. Senator Kirsten Gillibrand points to *The Invisible War* as her inspiration to create the Military Justice Improvement Act. In her 2014 memoir, *Off the Sidelines: Raise Your Voice, Change the World*, Gillibrand writes, "Nothing in my life . . . prepared me for what I saw in that film. . . . Whatever it took, I had to help bring justice to these survivors, and I needed to work to prevent further crimes." (Aguayo 2019, 89)

The *Gasland* study makes, in my view, a very convincing case for the impact of a politically oriented documentary film on community social action, particularly when the film is deployed within a BNF-like screening campaign. The account of the impact of *The Invisible War* at the level of federal policy is similarly, though for different reasons, convincing and impressive. In neither case, of course, have we heard the last word on the subject. Fracking continues, and so no doubt does rape in the military, not to mention in other contexts explored in subsequent Kirby Dick films (*The Hunting Ground* [2015], about college campuses; *On the Record* [2020], about the recording industry). But for the activist filmmaker, every victory matters.

Thus as we come to the end of this book, we turn to the question of the social and political impact of BNF films, of whether they too have "made a difference." Brave New Films avoids survey-based impact studies but produces their own in-house reports on both individual films and on a given year's output of films and videos. I will use these reports to discuss the kinds of impact BNF sees itself as having had and to think about, in David Meyer's words, the more "complex and veiled" effects of their work.

Visible Results

I will start by summarizing some of the visible effects that Brave New Films has claimed as resulting from their films. By "visible" I mean that those effects have registered in the public culture in some way, as opposed to (or over and above) having structural effects that are largely invisible. I note first that, with very few exceptions, Greenwald almost never credits these results to the impact of a BNF film alone; instead he emphasizes a film's role in a larger campaign involving networks of partners and on-the-ground actions. I also note that, in some cases, some of the successful outcomes appear within the films, as there is already a movement underway that the film is joining and furthering, while others are noted in the impact reports or other sources after the fact. But again, Greenwald virtually never claims sole credit for these successes and is always careful to give clear credit to all the groups who have played a role in both the film and the events.

Greenwald has used the phrase "upstairs-downstairs model" to describe the two levels at which he aims for impact (in Haynes and Littler 2007; SBO interview, November 20, 2020). "Upstairs" refers to efforts to change policy and possibly generate legislation at high levels of governmental authority, as in the *Invisible War* example just noted. "Downstairs" refers to the effort to galvanize action and produce recognizable results at the grassroots level of communities, municipalities, and so forth, as in the *Gasland* example. I'll use this division to organize the instances of visible impact of BNF films.

Starting with the downstairs level, the visible effects may be gathered under the heading of "resistance," in the fairly simple sense that some powerful entity was trying to impose some harmful action on a particular group or community, and the BNF film participated in a successful pushback campaign. At the end of the film *Unconstitutional*, for example, we saw that a significant number of communities resisted the implementation of the Patriot Act and declared themselves "Civil Liberties Safe Zones." Other examples include the cancellation, after the release of *Outfoxed*, of a Democratic presidential debate in 2004 that was to have been hosted by Fox News (*Outfoxed Effect—10 Years Later*).[7] With respect to *Wal-Mart*, which details the way a Walmart store can impoverish a community, we saw within the film several communities successfully resisting the opening of a Walmart store, and we learn about others later—for example, how Walmart pulled out of a British scheme in the wake of a major campaign against them that prominently involved the film (Haynes 2007, 11n8). In 2011 BNF released a video series about labor issues called *Meet the New American Sweatshop* and claimed (along with their partner groups) a major victory: "The carwash workers in Santa Monica, CA, won a labor contract making Bonus Carwash the first unionized carwash in the country" (2011 Annual Report). In 2012 BNF released *Koch Brothers*

Exposed, documenting, among other things, the way the Koch brothers manipulated a school board election in Wake County, North Carolina, to achieve resegregation of the local schools. The film was part of a successful campaign to unseat that school board in the next election. In 2013 Brave New Films started making a series of videos about mass incarceration. Several of the videos focus on the problem of private, for-profit prisons, and as part of this effort BNF joined a coalition that successfully stopped the GEO group, "a notoriously abusive private prison company," from having its name on Florida Atlantic University's football stadium (Brave New Films 2016).

Turning to the upstairs side, a number of BNF films and videos have been reported to influence legislation. For example, with respect to the war profiteering documented in *Iraq for Sale*, there was a Senate committee investigation in 2006 of some of the charges made in the film (Finke 2006), and the House subsequently passed a bill called the War Profiteering Prevention Act (Haynes 2007, 12n8). Next, as part of the mass incarceration series, BNF made a series of videos about alternatives to incarceration, which were shown to Governor Cuomo's staff in the New York State legislature during their budget-writing process. The results included an additional $7 million and a dedicated funding stream for alternatives-to-incarceration projects. The film was also part of a briefing to state legislators in Texas, and favorable bills were also passed there. Also in this series, a video called *Yes on Prop 64* is described as having played a critical role in the successful campaign to decriminalize marijuana in California. And after BNF released *Making a Killing*, about the terrible toll of gun violence in the United States, a proposed bill allowing guns on college campuses was defeated in Florida, and the Educators' Pension Fund announced that teachers would be allowed to divest their money from gun companies in the portfolio (2015 Annual Report).

The role of the film in all of these cases is quite variable. The company does not try to quantify their contribution in each case and, indeed, makes an effort to balance the contribution of the film with the contribution of all the other parties—partners, community groups, organizations that were already at work when Brave New Films came on the scene, and so on. But they did make a particular contribution, a "powerful text" that conveyed truthful information and strong affect in a striking form, that could be manageably inserted into people's busy work schedules, and that reasonable observers might agree contributed to whatever positive outcome emerged.

Contributing to Movement Infrastructure

The idea that documentaries may have not only the kinds of tangible "impact" just sketched for Brave New Films but also the broader structural or systemic effects as a result of their activism has been widely recognized by media scholars in the recent literature on activist filmmaking. Angela Aguayo writes: "Documentary circulation creates something new in politics, a space I call a *documentary commons*, which continually grows, takes shape, and expands its participatory capacities" (2019, x). Caty Borum Chattoo explains how documentary work both draws on and contributes to "civil society": "Documentaries that interrogate social problems and inequities are enriched by civil society networks . . . already working deeply on the ground. . . . In return, nongovernmental organizations (NGOs) can be newly empowered when they work with documentaries as collaborators, partners, grassroots organizers, and message amplifiers" (2020, 71–72). John Haynes, writing of Brave New Films in particular, describes the ways BNF's distribution system, including the use of "dense networks" of activist organizations along with house parties and other face-to-face screening practices, are both grounded in, and contribute to, "a participatory ethic," which he sees as having been waning in American society (2007, 10).

Much of chapter 3 was devoted to this point. I laid out how Brave New Films draws on networks of groups and organizations to get maximum circulation for their films, but by the same token we can say that all of this networking activity contributes to the health of a social-movement infrastructure that remains active and available even when social movements are not in a phase of public activism. Similarly, I discussed the ways BNF maximizes internet-based tools to get the widest circulation for their films, but we can also say that their internet activism promotes the growth of a politically conscious counterpublic, again part of a latent infrastructure for potential social movements.

Here I want to push that point a bit further. In their work on recent developments in the political documentary, Angela Aguayo, Caty Borum

Chattoo, and others have emphasized how the new documentary has drawn in previously marginalized communities—women, queer subjects, Indigenous communities, communities of color, and so forth. Not only are these groups and categories more represented than before; they are also playing more active roles in producing their own representations. Although Brave New Films does not claim to be representing any particular community, we have seen that it is committed to making hard-hitting films about systemic racism in the United States and that it has made a significant number of full-length films and videos on the subject. Going further, one can perhaps say BNF is making a particular contribution in this area, as many of their films and videos on the subject of racism make a point of showing the intersection between racism and other forms of inequality: between racism and capitalism, as in the mass incarceration series, and between racism and the subversion of democracy, in the films about voter suppression and other attacks on constitutional rights. Here, then, we can say that BNF seeks not only to mobilize a generic activist counterpublic but also to foster a broader intersectionality of both diverse groups and diverse political agendas.

Shifting the Narrative

Recall here the discussion of Brave New Films as part of the alternative media, challenging the mainstream media versions of political realities. Alternative media offer what they see as more truthful versions of those realities, and they hope to persuade the American public of those truths. This, then, is BNF's most ambitious goal—"to shift attitudes on an issue and impact the mainstream narrative" (Brave New Films 2016, 3)—and when it works, it represents their most ambitious claim of "impact." Here, then, we move beyond specific victories; or, rather, specific victories become indexes of larger shifts in "media narratives" and the "national consensus."

An early example of BNF success along these lines was a campaign built around the film *Rethink Afghanistan* (2009), designed to stop a planned escalation of the war in Afghanistan early in the Obama administration and to start a process of de-escalation. As described in the impact report (Brave New Foundation 2012), Greenwald and his allies first put together a large coalition of progressive organizations to work on the project. (The work of all these groups is central to the campaign, and Greenwald is careful to emphasize that throughout the report.) They then launched an extended and carefully sequenced campaign across multiple media platforms: an intensive blogging effort, followed by a series of short video debates over the war, followed by a letter to President Obama signed by prominent progressive academics and organizations, followed by the timed release of chapters of the *Rethink Afghanistan* documentary over the next few months, followed by a massive Facebook campaign, all in 2009. The antiwar numbers started rising in the polls (3), and on July 24, 2010, *Newsweek* published a cover story called *Rethinking Afghanistan*, echoing the name of the film and further boosting the growing opposition to the war. By 2012 (when the report was published), according to various independent polls, public opinion about the war in Afghanistan had shifted from a majority pro-war (63 percent) to a majority antiwar (78 percent) over the period of the campaign. The report summarizes: "Thanks in large part to our work changing the media narrative, the national conversation has finally shifted against the war" (1).

We know today that neither changing the media narrative nor changing the national conversation actually stopped the war in Afghanistan, which went on for another nine years (until 2021, the year I write this). When I asked Greenwald in 2019 about any disappointments in his career with Brave New Films, the first thing he said was that the war in Afghanistan was still going on. But one can only forge ahead and keep fighting.

A second example of an attempt to use the work of Brave New Films to influence public opinion on a large scale was their campaign against mass incarceration, as summarized in a report called *Mass Incarceration: A Study on Building Capacity for Institutional Change in America's Unjust Prison System* (Brave New Films 2016). Again headlining the phrase "shifting the narrative" (3), they launched a multiyear campaign to "highlight the waste and injustice of the current jail and prison system while pointing the way to fairer, more effective alternatives" (4). Partnering with a large number of groups already working on this issue, they produced more than fifty videos over a three-year period, releasing them over social media and in screenings.[8] Under the heading "Impact" they list, among other things, a huge number of video views (29 million); over twelve hundred screenings; almost seven hundred press hits; and a number of awards for one or another video in the series (2). They also list "coverage in major press outlets," including *Time* magazine, the *Washington Post*, the *Guardian*, and more (3). Finally, at the bottom of each page they list one or two "victories" tied to specific videos.

Unlike with the report on the Afghanistan campaign, they do not offer public opinion polls, and/or statistics about the trending rate of incarceration in the United States, that could have supported a claim about shifting the weight of public opinion over that period. Thinking, then, about what it might mean for them to say that they were "shifting the narrative" with this campaign, it seemed to me that they were using the specific "victories" in the report not only as self-contained success stories, but as indexes of a larger change in the narrative. Thus, the victories listed at the bottom of each page show various ways that given films within the overall campaign achieved some kind of success, whether "breaking through" into the mainstream media (*Safekeepers*), or being part of a successful push-back campaign (*To Prison for Poverty*), or playing a role in the passage of good legislation (*How Texas Shut Down a Prison*) or the expiration of bad legislation (*To Prison for Pregnancy*), and so on. Moreover, the victories are presented in chronological order, so as one moves through the pages of the report and the successes build up, one may get a sense of progress in shifting the larger narrative about crime and punishment in America.

Unlike with the Afghanistan case, there does actually seem to be some timely progress in this area. Five years after the BNF impact report, a Pew Research Center report headlined "America's Incarceration Rate Falls to Lowest Level since 1995" shows a modest but consistent decline in the US incarceration rate for the period from 2008 (the peak) to 2019 (Gramlich 2021). It seems fair to give Brave New Films, along with all of the other organizations working on this issue, some credit for this outcome.

Finally, I want to suggest that a similar argument can tentatively be made with respect to *Suppressed*. *Suppressed* was not part of an extended campaign in the way *Rethink Afghanistan* and the mass incarceration video series were. Thus, it might seem excessive to promote the role of one thirty-eight-minute documentary film in the spectacular electoral successes of Georgia, including both the Democratic presidential win in 2020 and, in 2021, the successful Democratic campaign for two Senate seats in a state that had overwhelmingly voted Republican for decades. These results were brought about by the massive on-the-ground work of multiple organizations, many of them led and populated by Black women activists and spearheaded by the charismatic and indefatigable Stacey Abrams (Herndon 2020; see also Walsh 2021).

It takes nothing away from all this to insert the film into the story in ways that are particular to the kind of contribution a film like this, with its social media reach and all its partnering and screening operations, could make.[9] When Greenwald started working on *Suppressed* in late 2018, the concept of "voter suppression" was hardly an issue on everyone's lips. Moreover, the electoral politics of the state of Georgia were not at that point front-page news in most parts of the country, nor was it likely that the average American citizen, even among the small minority that follows the national news, was paying much attention to arcane state-level electoral machinations in Georgia. As with a lot of Greenwald's work, then, some of the impact came from coming into the scene early, with high intensity, and thus moving people's attention to what was at that point a relatively unknown issue. We heard several times in this book about how shocked people were to learn about what was going on.

Because of the massive grassroots, legal, and media work by many different organizations, Georgia quickly became national news. At the same time, Greenwald kept up an extremely active campaign for *Suppressed* on social media, as well as with the screening program, in both cases—I suggest—reaching publics (especially youth) that might not have been reached through mainstream media. By the time of the presidential election, voter suppression was much more widely recognized as an issue, and people began paying attention to it in their own state and local contexts. And thus perhaps it is not entirely unreasonable to say that *Suppressed* played a role, in its own way, in changing the media narrative, the national conversation, and perhaps even the 2020 electoral outcome itself.

Yet despite, or possibly because of, these victories, it seems as if the practice of voter suppression has only gotten worse since the election. More states have passed more suppression laws than before, and in a more brazen manner. I turn then to some brief conclusions about the future, and how Brave New Films, political documentary, and alternative media in general help us think about it.

A Very Brief Conclusion

The future seems to me extraordinarily shaky, but I want to end by reaffirming the great importance of alternative media, and the role of Brave New Films and all the other critical documentarians within that zone of the public culture. Given the commitment of documentary film to truth-telling and realism, this seems to me a very important development in and of itself. If the emergence of Fox News and other right-wing media represented a major, and highly destabilizing, shift in the public culture, the emergence of the political documentary represented a significant challenge to that shift. In other words, I am suggesting that perhaps the largest claim for "impact" that might be made for Brave New Films begins with the important role they played in the takeoff and growth of the political documentary "movement" as a whole. This movement in turn has played a major role in staking out and expanding a counterpublic space of truth-telling, and in putting ongoing pressure on the mainstream media to start acknowledging the truth.

But we cannot count on the continuing growth and artistic/journalistic independence of this movement. I opened my *New York Times* on December 26, 2020, and found a story, on the front page of the business section, headlined "Khashoggi as Subject Is Hard Sell." It tells the story of the difficulties encountered by filmmaker Bryan Fogel when he sought to find a distributor for his film *The Dissident* (2020). *The Dissident* is about the murder, with the apparent direct involvement of Crown Prince Mohammed bin Salman of Saudi Arabia, of Jamal Khashoggi, a Saudi Arabian dissident and *Washington Post* journalist. Netflix had distributed an earlier film by Fogel, called *Icarus* (2017), that had won an Academy Award. Yet Netflix did not bid to distribute *The Dissident*, and many of the other major streaming services declined as well. The *Times* reporter made a point of noting that Netflix had recently signed a multipicture deal with a Saudi Arabian film company. And in an earlier incident in which Netflix had quashed a sitcom episode that criticized Prince Mohammed after Khashoggi's death, Reed Hastings, the chief executive of Netflix, is quoted as saying, "We're not trying to do 'truth to power.' We're trying to entertain" (Sperling 2020).

It is not clear how much of a trend this story represents. It has always been difficult for documentaries to get commercial distribution; that was

Greenwald's point in turning to the nonprofit model back in 2004. But as the reporter and others pointed out, it is extremely unusual for a director who won an Oscar to have a hard time finding a distributor for his or her next film. Thus, it is hard not to feel some concern that this may be a forecast of declining support for the critical documentary.

At the same time, as I said in the introduction, we must remember to keep the ongoing movement activism in focus as well, both inside and outside the films. The films tell hard and unpleasant truths about the darkest sides of American society—capitalist greed, racist violence, fascist efforts to subvert democracy. But they refuse to leave us depressed and disheartened; they always end with some kind of victory and call us to action. The films thus embody, and this book has tried to embody, the complicated inspiration of Gramsci's famous dictum "Pessimism of the intellect, optimism of the will." Or, as the provocative poet and activist Maya Angelou put it, "Life's a bitch. You've got to go out and kick ass."

Notes

Introduction

1   I use the terms *resistance* and (involvement in) *social movements* in free variation. One could tease out some distinctions between them, but I haven't found it necessary for purposes of this book.

2   The quote is also attributed to playwright Moss Hart.

3   I have searched for this quote extensively and I can't find the reference. But it must be out there somewhere—I can't have made it up.

4   The exact quote is "If maximum social impact is to bring about needed legislation, why not spend money on lobbyists rather than films?"

5   Grierson professed to be "on the left," but his films have been heavily criticized for avoiding any political critique (Winston 1995; Nick Fraser 2019). Nonetheless, the sympathetic focus on workers of all kinds in those films fit in with the growing (left) insistence on the centrality of labor, and the humanity of workers, in the industrialized capitalist system.

6   As film buffs will immediately know, *The Battle of Algiers* was not a documentary, but it aspired to be as true as possible to the historical facts, and it borrowed many stylistic devices from documentary film.

7   There were also important technological developments that increased both the portability and the quality of equipment and thus facilitated increased production.

8   One could also look at the outcome of this process as the creation and self-creation of a self-conscious documentary "scene" that set itself apart not only from the mainstream media (see the next chapter), but also from the wild and seemingly undisciplined proliferation of do-it-yourself nonfiction video on the internet. Thanks to John Caldwell for emphasizing this point.

9 "Protests against the Iraq War," Wikipedia, accessed August 29, 2021, https://en.wikipedia.org/wiki/Protests_against_the_Iraq_War.

10 *Uncovered* appears to have been the first anti–Iraq War film to come out after the invasion. Wanting to respond quickly, Greenwald brought out a short version in November 2003, only eight months after the March invasion (*Uncovered: The Whole Truth about the Iraq War*), and a longer version (*Uncovered: The War on Iraq*) the following year (Kellner 2010, 60).

11 Their commitment to this model has meant that their films are often unknown, even within the relatively small world of documentary film fans, as the films do not appear on TV or in theaters. But, as I will discuss in the final chapter, their "impact" does not depend on widespread recognition.

12 See also the videos *Citizen Tube Interview* (2008) and *Our Story* (2015).

13 For non-social-science people reading this book, the "actor" of social theory is a generic term for a social person in the abstract and is not to be confused with actors in the film or stage sense.

14 Deborah Gordon writes about the Ruth Benedict Collective briefly in *Women Writing Culture* (1995).

1. Brave New Films in the Mediascape

1 One level I will not address in this book is the level of individual independent filmmakers. Some have been mentioned already, particularly if they made an award-winning film (e.g., Michael Moore, Charles Ferguson). Independent filmmakers were covered extensively in *Not Hollywood* (Ortner 2013b), but here I mention a few favorites among documentarians, along with Moore and Ferguson—Emile de Antonio, Kirby Dick, Ava DuVernay, Alex Gibney, Spike Lee, Lucy Walker—as they are part of this book's larger context.

2 The study of ethnographic film would go on to develop and evolve in important ways, beyond the scope of this book. To follow this thread see, e.g., Barbash and Taylor 1997; Rouch 2003; Banks and Ruby 2011; and MacDonald 2013.

3 For an excellent recent example see Rouse, Jackson, and Frederick 2016.

4 By now they seem to have developed a more conventional hierarchical organization, but they describe themselves on their website as "a collaborative community." It is hard to know more about how they operate without doing the ethnography.

5 The fellows are paid. The interns are covered by scholarships awarded through their home colleges or universities.

6 Some of the coproducers are on the regular staff, while others may be hired on a contract basis for a particular film.

2. Critical Agency

1. For a thoughtful discussion of what anthropology can contribute to the critical understanding of post-truth, see Ho and Cavanaugh 2019 and the set of essays in the Vital Topics Forum of the *American Anthropologist* to which their article was an introduction.

2. The completed video is called *Sophrosyne Mental Health* (2020).

3. See also Espinosa 1979 on the political significance of "imperfect cinema."

4. In fact, Greenwald told me that there were more suppression mechanisms, and they had to leave some out as the film got too long and too complicated.

5. Greenwald had executive-produced one earlier film under the new Brave New Films company name, *Unprecedented: The 2000 Presidential Election* (2002), directed by Joan Sekler and Richard Ray Pérez.

6. The film was written up in a major story in the *New York Times Magazine* (Boynton 2004).

7. Greenwald sees legislation as important, but not as "systemic change" (email, February 28, 2021). This represents Omar's take on "systemic."

8. For some recent anthropological perspectives on systemic racism, see, e.g., Ralph and Chance 2014; Burton 2015; B. Williams 2015; Vargas 2015; Ralph 2017; and Partis 2019.

9. The film was directed by Nonny de la Peña and executive-produced by Robert Greenwald.

10. The film was directed by Joan Sekler and Richard Ray Pérez and executive-produced by Robert Greenwald.

11. In retrospect this appears to be a precursor to the right-wing storming of the US Capitol in 2021 to disrupt the certification of the election lost by Donald Trump.

12. Greenwald updated the film to capture the effects of the COVID-19 pandemic on the voting process and produced a version called *Suppressed 2020: The Fight to Vote* (2020).

13. David Koch died in 2019.

14. Speaking personally, I found the documentary about the Koch brothers the most frightening of the BNF films along these lines. In conjunction with watching that film, I also read two books that deepened the sense of the serious possibility of a fascist takeover taking place out of sight and under the radar, journalist Jane Mayer's *Dark Money: The Hidden History of the Billionaires behind the Rise of the Radical Right* (2016; Mayer also appears in the film), and historian Nancy MacLean's *Democracy in Chains: A Deep History of the Radical Right's Stealth Plan for America* (2017).

15   There are multiple versions of this "confession." This one is attributed to the
Holocaust Memorial Day Trust: see "First they came," Wikipedia, accessed
May 5, 2022, https://en.wikipedia.org/wiki/First_they_came_. . . .

3. Networked Agency

1   The references here are in every case just tiny selections from very large bodies of academic/scholarly literature, simply meant to give the reader a starting
point or two. In addition to those bodies of work and to the writings of some
scholar-activists already cited (Graeber, Juris, Appel, etc.), there are also the
important and inspiring writings of full-time activists (e.g., Garza 2014; Taylor
2017; Solomon and Rankin 2019).

2   These quotations are from the back cover of BNF's 2018 annual report.

3   The relationship between the company Twitter account and Greenwald's
personal account is not clear.

4   Patricia Aufderheide makes extensive use of the idea of "publics" in an article
on films about the Iraq War. In this context she asks about the different publics that get constructed by films on this subject that are made from different
points of view (2007).

5   Good Pitch homepage, accessed November 21, 2020, https://goodpitch.org.

6   Art Haywood, Facebook post, November 2, 2020, https://www.facebook.com
/art.haywood.3.

7   For my project on independent film (Ortner 2013b), I was able to attend over
a hundred screenings with Q&As, because most of the screenings were held in
Los Angeles, one of the epicenters (along with New York) of the independent
film movement. The Brave New Films screenings, by contrast, are spread all
over the country, and I did not have either the time or the budget to travel out
of state to observe them. I went to as many screenings in the Los Angeles area
as I could get to, until live screenings were discontinued due to the COVID-19
pandemic.

8   Anne Phillips had notified the minister that I was coming and asked if it would
be acceptable for me to be there.

9   The series covers a wide range of issues, including voter mobilization, climate
change, the school-to-prison pipeline, reproductive health, immigrant rights,
and mental health (this list from the website).

10   It is not clear why the turnout in the West Adams community theater was so
poor. The organizer said she had had about thirty RSVPs and was quite upset
about the small number of people who showed up.

11   Director of the Faith Outreach Program Tahil Sharma spoke at a BNF staff
meeting about this pastor, whom he described as "very progressive," saying

that "he went out in the streets and tried to calm people down during the Rodney King events." Tahil described the church as a whole as "very progressive, involved in social justice work" (field notes, September 18, 2019).

12 It is not clear why a state representative from Alabama was present; I'm guessing he was a friend of the organizer. But as an elected African American official, he certainly had much to say of relevance to the film and the event.

13 Although I did not have the opportunity to observe multiple student screenings, I base this point on my own experience as a teacher of undergraduates.

14 Closer to home, a BNF video called *The Call to Sanctuary: How to Create Safety in Your Community*, includes a sequence at a town meeting in a community near my university in which local citizens are debating a proposal to declare the city a sanctuary city for undocumented immigrants. I learned from a colleague who was there that the meeting had been harassed by right-wing groups, but the proposal passed by a close vote at 1 a.m. We don't see this in the video, the main point of which is to inform individuals and communities of their rights under the Constitution with respect to immigration law, and to detail all the things people and groups can legally do to protect undocumented immigrants from the overreach of ICE (Immigration and Customs Enforcement) and the increasingly right-wing US state.

15 I use the past tense here because, tragically, both died young. Juris died in 2020, at the age of forty-nine, after a long battle with brain cancer, and Graeber died suddenly in 2020, at the age of fifty-nine, of acute pancreatitis.

4. Affective Agency

1 For a quick introduction, see Gregg and Seigworth 2010. For affect theory specifically within anthropology, see, e.g., Rutherford 2016; Mazzarella 2010; and Mankekar 2015. On "affective labor," see Hardt 1999.

2 Borum Chattoo 2020, 103, has a brief discussion of characters in documentary.

3 In an article called "The Voice of Documentary" (2005), Bill Nichols raises a number of important questions about the believability of characters in documentaries. The arguments are complex and would need to be addressed in a separate article.

4 Most of the people to be discussed here were interviewed by coproducer Casey Cooper Johnson or by Greenwald himself. I would have liked to join some actual interviewing shoots, to see and get a feel for how the producer interacts with the interviewees. For example, Casey made some thoughtful comments about the benefit of having a two-person crew so that he could concentrate on the quality of his interaction with the interviewee: "I had a good cinematographer who could light things well, and be more focused on

setting up the cameras while I'm trying to get to know this person who . . . [I'm] finally meet[ing] in person for the first time. To try and get them comfortable to do an interview before we run off and disappear again." But with the exception of one telephone interview between Greenwald and one of the experts, which I sat in on in Greenwald's office, I did not have the opportunity in this case to do the live ethnography.

5   Outreach director Anne Phillips was kind enough to share a batch of this material with me, as long as I do not publish the names of the sources. All identifying information has been removed.

6   In a famous example, Barbara Kopple, director of *Harlan County, U.S.A.*, brought some of the musicians whose music had been heard on the soundtrack, as well as some of the coal miners from the film, onto the stage at the Lincoln Center Film Festival in 1976 (Kaplan 1984, 219).

5. The Impact Question, and Conclusions

1   I would also guess that the genre itself has gained in popularity—that more people watch documentaries and fewer people dislike them. But I have not seen any hard data to that effect.

2   The two most prominent of these impact research organizations are the Media Impact Project at the University of Southern California (USC), and the Center for Media and Social Impact at American University in Washington, DC.

3   These are exceptionally high numbers. The authors of the report call the 84 percent figure "astounding."

4   Anthropologist Steven Caton writes of being deeply impressed by the film *Lawrence of Arabia* at the age of thirteen, so much so that he wrote an entire book about that one film more than thirty years later (1999, 1–2). Producer Nick Fraser writes of seeing *The Sorrow and the Pity* with his mother as a young man in his twenties, and recalls the experience, decades later, as the time when he came to understand the power of truth in documentary (2019, 8–10).

5   This is not to dismiss survey research wholesale. As psychologist Abigail Stewart argues (personal communication), many of the problems with survey research come from poor research design rather than from the methodology itself.

6   It lost to *Inside Job* (2010, dir. Charles Ferguson), a truly brilliant film (in my opinion) about the extremely risky, and sometimes criminal, financial behavior on Wall Street that led up to the near-crash of the stock market in 2008.

7   Examples are drawn mostly from BNF impact reports but in some cases, as cited, from other sources.

8   They note "50+ videos" on page 2 of the report but "35 in total" on page 5.
     I assume the difference is made up by drawing in videos that were relevant
     from other campaigns and/or were excerpted from existing full-length films
     they had made. This is common practice at the company (Greenwald talks
     about "slicing and dicing" his films for social media), and it makes sense given
     that all of the themes they address are closely interrelated.

9   Two other—very good, in my opinion—documentaries about voter suppres-
     sion also came out in this period: *All In: The Fight for Democracy* (2020), also
     about the Georgia case; and *Slay the Dragon* (2019), about gerrymandering in
     Michigan. They too surely contributed in their own ways to the "impact."

Filmography

NOTE: ALL BNF FILMS AND VIDEOS ARE AVAILABLE ON YOUTUBE UNLESS
OTHERWISE NOTED.

All In: The Fight for Democracy. 2020. Directed by Liz Garbus and Lisa Cortés.
   Produced by Stacey Abrams, Liz Garbus, Lisa Cortés, and Dan Cogan.
   Amazon.
An American Family. 1973. Produced by Craig Gilbert. WNET New York.
Avatar. 2009. Directed by James Cameron. Produced by James Cameron
   and Jon Landau. 20th Century Fox, Lightstorm Entertainment, Dune
   Entertainment, Ingenious Film Partners.
The Bail Trap: American Ransom (video). 2018. Brave New Films.
The Battle of Algiers. 1966. Directed by Gillo Pontecorvo. Produced by Antonio
   Musu and Saadi Yacef. Rizzoli.
The Battle of Chile. 1975. Directed by Patricio Guzmán. A coproduction with
   Instituto Cubano del Arte y Industría Cinematograficos (ICAIC) and
   Chris Marker.
The Black Panthers: Vanguard of the Revolution. 2015. Directed by Stanley Nel-
   son Jr. Produced by Laurens Grant and Stanley Nelson Jr. PBS.
BNS_Robert_Greenwald_Discussions_v4_Final_Master (video). 2018. Vimeo.
   https://vimeo.com/242793270. Accessed November 29, 2019.
Bowling for Columbine. 2002. Directed by Michael Moore. Produced by Mi-
   chael Moore, Kathleen Glynn, Jim Czarnecki, Charles Bishop, Michael
   Donovan, and Kurt Engfehr. United Artists, Alliance Atlantis, Salter
   Street Films, and Dog Eat Dog Films.
Breaking Down Bail: Debunking Common Bail Myths (video). 2017. Brave New
   Films.

California's Punishment Economy: The State's $20 Billion Industry (video). 2019. Brave New Films.

The Call to Sanctuary: How to Create Safety in Your Community (video). 2018. Brave New Films.

The CBC: Fighting for Black America (video). 2020. Brave New Films.

Citizen Tube Interview with Robert Greenwald (video). 2008. YouTube. Accessed November 29, 2019. https://www.youtube.com/watch?v =WQCXCJbMRrM&app=desktop.

Columbia Revolt. 1968. Produced and directed by Newsreel.

Contagion. 2011. Directed by Steven Soderbergh. Produced by Michael Shamberg, Stacey Sher, and Gregory Jacobs. Participant Media.

DEA Boss to Agents: Target Black Neighborhoods, Avoid White Suburbs (video). 2015. Brave New Films.

A Deal with the Devil: Plea Deals (video). 2018. Brave New Films.

The Dissident. 2020. Directed by Bryan Fogel. Produced by Bryan Fogel, Jake Swantko, Mark Monroe, and Thor Halverssen. Briarcliff Entertainment.

Fahrenheit 9/11. 2004. Directed by Michael Moore. Produced by Michael Moore, Jim Czarnecki, Kathleen Glynn, Monica Hampton, Harvey Weinstein, and Bob Weinstein. Lionsgate Films.

Families Torn Apart: America's Deadly Immigration Policy (video). 2020. Brave New Films.

Food, Inc. 2009. Directed by Robert Kenner. Produced by Robert Kenner and Elise Pearlstein. Participant Media.

Four Little Girls. 1997. Directed by Spike Lee. Produced by Spike Lee, Sam Pollard, and Daphne A. McWilliams. Forty Acres & a Mule, Filmworks, and HBO.

Gasland. 2010. Directed by Josh Fox. Produced by Trish Adlesic, Molly Gandour, Josh Fox, and David Roma. HBO.

Harlan County, U.S.A. 1976. Directed by Barbara Kopple. Produced by Barbara Kopple. Cinema 5.

Healing Trauma (video series). 2019. Brave New Films.

Hearts and Minds. 1974. Directed by Peter Davis. Produced by Bert Schneider and Peter Davis. Rainbow Releasing and Warner Brothers.

Hoop Dreams. 1994. Directed by Steve James. Produced by Steve James, Peter Gilbert, and Frederick Marx. Kartemquin Films.

The Hour of the Furnaces: Notes and Testimonies on Neocolonialism, Violence, and Liberation. 1968. Directed by Fernando Solanas and Octavio Getino. Produced by Edgardo Pallero and Fernando Solanas. Grupo Cine Liberación and Solanas Productions.

How Texas Shut Down a Prison (video). 2014. Brave New Films.

The Hunting Ground. 2015. Directed by Kirby Dick. Produced by Amy Ziering. The Weinstein Company.

Icarus. 2017. Directed by Bryan Fogel. Produced by Dan Cogan, Bryan Fogel, David Fialkow, and Jim Swartz. Netflix.

Immigrant Prisons (video). 2108. Brave New Films.

Immigrant Stories: Doctors and Teachers Speak Out (video). 2019. Brave New Films.

An Inconvenient Truth. 2006. Directed by Davis Guggenheim. Produced by Laurie David, Lawrence Bender, and Scott Z. Burns. Participant Media.

Inside Job. 2010. Directed by Charles Ferguson. Produced by Audrey Marrs and Charles Ferguson. Sony Pictures Classics.

In the Year of the Pig. 1969. Directed by Emile de Antonio. Produced by John Attlee, Emile de Antonio, Terry Morrone, and Orville Schell. Emilio de Antonio Productions and Turin Film Productions.

The Invisible War. 2012. Directed by Kirby Dick. Produced by Amy Ziering and Tanner King Barlow. Chain Camera Pictures.

Iraq for Sale: The War Profiteers. 2006. Directed by Robert Greenwald. Brave New Films.

Judas and the Black Messiah. 2021. Directed by Shaka King. Produced by Charles D. King, Ryan Coogler, and Shaka King. MACRO, Participant, Bron Creative, and Proximity.

Koch Brothers Exposed. 2012. Directed by Robert Greenwald. Brave New Films.

Lawrence of Arabia. 1962. Directed by David Lean. Produced by Sam Spiegel. Horizon Pictures.

Little Children. 2006. Directed by Todd Field. Produced by Todd Field, Albert Berger, and Ron Yerxa. Bona Fide Productions and Standard Film Company.

Little Miss Sunshine. 2006. Directed by Jonathan Dayton and Valerie Faris. Produced by Marc Turtletaub, David T. Friendly, Peter Saraf, Albert Berger, and Ron Yerxa. Big Beach Films, Bona Fide Productions, Deep River Productions, and Third Gear Productions.

Maddie's Grandparents: A Preventable COVID Tragedy (video). 2020. Brave New Films.

Making a Killing: Guns, Greed, and the NRA. 2016. Directed by Robert Greenwald. Brave New Films.

Manufacturing Consent: Noam Chomsky and the Media. 1992. Directed by Mark Achbar and Peter Wintonick. Produced by Mark Achbar, Adam Symansky, and Peter Wintonick. Zeitgeist Films.

Medium Cool. 1969. Directed by Haskell Wexler. Produced by Tully Friedman, Haskell Wexler, and Jerrold Wexler. H & J Productions.

Meet the Nazis That Patrol the U.S.-Mexico Border (video). 2015. Brave New Films.

Memories of Underdevelopment. 1968. Directed by Tomás Gutiérrez Alea. Produced by Miguel Mendoza.

Mental Health Experts and Donald Trump (video). 2018. Brave New Films.

Milwaukee 53206. 2016. Directed by Keith McQuirter. Produced by Keith McQuirter, Katie Taber, and Adam S. Miller. Transform Films Inc.

Minding the Gap. 2018. Directed by Bing Liu. Produced by Bing Liu and Diane Moy Quon. Kartemquin Films.

Native Land. 1942. Directed by Leo Hurwitz and Paul Strand. Produced by Leo Hurvitz. Frontier Films.

Obama's America. 2016. Directed by Dinesh D'Souza and John Sullivan. Produced by Gerald R. Molen and Doug Sain. Obama's America Foundation.

On the Record. 2020. Directed by Kirby Dick and Amy Ziering. Produced by Kirby Dick, Amy Herdy, Jamie Rogers, and Amy Ziering. HBO.

Our Story: Behind the Scenes with Brave New Films: Who We Are and What We Do: Ten Year Featurette (video). 2015. YouTube. Accessed November 29, 2019. https://www.youtube.com/watch?v=DLSneV-8u_U.

Outfoxed: Rupert Murdoch's War on Journalism. 2004. Directed by Robert Greenwald. Brave New Films.

Outfoxed Effect—10 Years Later. 2014. Brave New Films. YouTube. Accessed February 14, 2021. https://www.youtube.com/watch?v=_2i_HH54BPk.

The Panama Deception. 1992. Directed by Barbara Trent. Produced by David Kasper, Joanne Doroshow, and Nico Panigutti. Empowerment Project, Channel 4 Television Corporation, and Rhino Home Video.

Paris Is Burning. 1990. Directed by Jennie Livingston. Produced by Jennie Livingston and Barry Swimar. BBC Television, Miramax, Off-White Productions Inc., Prestige, and WNYC_TV.

Prison by the Numbers (video). 2014. Brave New Films.

Prisoner Gets a Bad Bargain: A Deal with the Devil. (Alternative title: *A Deal with the Devil: Plea Deals*) (video). 2018. Brave New Films.

Prison Profiteers: Six Institutions That Profit from the Police State (video). 2014. Brave New Films.

Racially Charged: America's Misdemeanor Problem. 2021. Directed by Robert Greenwald. Brave New Films.

Racism Is Real (video). 2016. Brave New Films.

Rethink Afghanistan. 2009. Directed by Robert Greenwald. Brave New Films.

Roger and Me. 1989. Directed by Michael Moore. Produced by Michael Moore. Warner Bros.

Safekeepers (video). 2012. Brave New Films.

Slay the Dragon. 2019. Directed by Christopher Durrance and Barak Goodman. Produced by Christopher Durrance and Barak Goodman. Magnolia Pictures and Participant Media.

Social Impact When the World Is Inside. 2020. Webinar moderated by Caitlin Boyle. DocNYC Pro. Accessed June 3, 2020. https://www.crowdcast.io/e/immersive-socialimpact/1.

Sophrosyne Mental Health (video). 2020. *Following Their Lead: Youth in Action* series. Brave New Films.

The Sorrow and the Pity. 1969. Directed by Marcel Ophuls. Produced by Alain de Sedouy and André Harris. Norddeutscher Rundfunk and radiodiffusion.

The Spanish Earth. 1937. Directed by Joris Ivens. Produced by Herman Shumlin. Contemporary Historians Inc.

Suppressed: The Fight to Vote. 2019. Directed by Robert Greenwald. Brave New Films.

Suppressed 2020: The Fight to Vote. 2020. Directed by Robert Greenwald. Brave New Films.

The Thin Blue Line. 1988. Directed by Errol Morris. Produced by Mark Lipson. Miramax.

The Three Burials of Melquiades Estrada. 2005. Directed by Tommy Lee Jones. Produced by Luc Besson, Michael Fitzgerald, and Pierre-Ange Le Pogam. EuropaCorp and The Javelina Film Company.

Time to Come Home: 20 Years Is Enough: End Life Imprisonment (video). 2019. Brave New Films.

Titicut Follies. 1967. Directed by Frederick Wiseman. Produced by Frederick Wiseman. Bridgewater Film.

To Prison for Poverty (video). 2016. Brave New Films.

To Prison for Pregnancy (video). 2016. Brave New Films.

Triumph of the Will. 1935. Directed by Leni Riefenstahl. Produced by Leni Riefenstahl.

Trump vs. Trump on Coronavirus (video). 2020. Brave New Films.

Trump vs. Trump on Putin and Russia (video). 2019. Brave New Films.

Unconstitutional: The War on our Civil Liberties. 2004. Directed by Nonny de la Peña. Executive-produced by Robert Greenwald. Public Interest Pictures.

Uncovered: The War on Iraq. 2004. Directed by Robert Greenwald. Brave New Films.

Uncovered: The Whole Truth about the Iraq War. 2003. Directed by Robert Greenwald. Brave New Films.

Unmanned: America's Drone Wars. 2013. Directed by Robert Greenwald. Brave New Films.

Unprecedented: The 2000 Presidential Election. 2002. Directed by Joan Sekler
   and Richard Ray Pérez. Executive-produced by Robert Greenwald.
   Shout! Factory.
Waiting for "Superman." 2010. Directed by Davis Guggenheim. Produced by
   Davis Guggenheim, Lesley Chilcott, and Michael Birtel. Participant
   Media.
Wal-Mart: The High Cost of Low Price. 2005. Directed by Robert Greenwald.
   Brave New Films.
War on Whistleblowers: Free Press and the National Security State. 2013. Directed
   by Robert Greenwald. Brave New Films.
Weather Underground. 2002. Directed by Sam Green and Bill Siegel. Produced
   by Sam Green, Carrie Lozano, Bill Siegel, and Mark Smolowitz. The Free
   History Project.
Xala. 1974. Directed by Ousmane Sembène. Produced by Filmi Domireve
   SNC.
Yes on Prop 64 (video). 2016. Brave New Films.
Youth Rise Texas (video). 2019. *Following Their Lead: Youth in Action* series.
   Brave New Films.

References

Abu-Lughod, Lila. 1995. "The Objects of Soap Opera: Egyptian Television and the Cultural Politics of Modernity." In *Worlds Apart: Modernity through the Prism of the Local,* edited by Daniel Miller, 190–210. London: Routledge.

Abu-Lughod, Lila. 2005. *Dramas of Nationhood: The Politics of Television in Egypt.* Chicago: University of Chicago Press.

Abu-Lughod, Lila. 2019. "The Courage of Truth: Making Anthropology Matter." Paper delivered at the Inaugural Lecture of Anthropology at KU Leuven, September 24, 2019. Typescript.

Aguayo, Angela J. 2019. *Documentary Resistance: Social Change and Participatory Media.* New York: Oxford University Press.

Alvarez, Sonia E., Evelina Dagnino, and Arturo Escobar, eds. 1998. *Cultures of Politics, Politics of Cultures: Re-visioning Latin American Social Movements.* Boulder, CO: Westview.

Anderson, Benedict. 1983. *Imagined Communities: Reflections on the Origin and Spread of Nationalism.* London: Verso.

Anderson, Carol. 2019. *One Person, No Vote: How Voter Suppression Is Destroying Our Democracy.* New York: Bloomsbury.

Appadurai, Arjun, ed. 1986. *The Social Life of Things: Commodities in Cultural Perspective.* Cambridge: Cambridge University Press.

Appadurai, Arjun. 1990. "Disjuncture and Difference in the Global Cultural Economy." *Public Culture* 2 (2): 1–24.

Appadurai, Arjun, and Carol A. Breckenridge. 1988. "Why Public Culture?" *Public Culture Bulletin* 1 (1): 5–9.

Appel, Hannah. 2014. "Occupy Wall Street and the Economic Imagination." *Cultural Anthropology* 29 (4): 602–25.

Arendt, Hannah. 1969. "Lying in Politics: Reflections on the Pentagon Papers." In *Crises of the Republic*, 1–48. New York: Harcourt Brace and Co.

Armstrong, David. 1981. *A Trumpet to Arms: Alternate Media in America*. Boston: South End.

Askew, Kelly, and Richard R. Wilk, eds. 2002. *The Anthropology of Media: A Reader*. Malden, MA: Blackwell.

Aufderheide, Patricia. 2007. "Your Country, My Country: How Films about the Iraq War Construct Publics." *Framework* 48 (2): 56–65.

Banks, Marcus, and Jay Ruby, eds. 2011. *Made to Be Seen: Perspectives on the History of Visual Anthropology*. Chicago: University of Chicago Press.

Barbash, Ilisa, and Lucien (Castaing) Taylor. 1997. *Cross-Cultural Filmmaking: A Handbook for Making Documentary and Ethnographic Films and Videos*. Berkeley: University of California Press.

Benson, Thomas W., and Brian J. Snee, eds. 2008. *The Rhetoric of the New Political Documentary*. Carbondale: University of Southern Illinois Press.

Bettig, Ronald V., and Jeanne Lynn Hall. 2008. "Outfoxing the Myth of the Liberal Media." In *The Rhetoric of the New Political Documentary*, edited by Thomas W. Benson and Brian J. Snee, 173–201. Carbondale: Southern Illinois University Press.

Blakley, Johanna, Grace Huang, Sheena Nahm, and Heesung Shin. n.d. *Changing Appetites and Changing Minds: Measuring the Impact of "Food, Inc."* Los Angeles: USC Annenberg Norman Lear Center: Media Impact Project. https://learcenter.org/wp-content/uploads/2016/06/Food-Inc-Summary-Report.pdf.

Blumenthal, Jerry, and Jennifer Rohrer. 1980. "'The Chicago Maternity Center Story' and The Kartemquin Collective." In *The Documentary Conscience: A Casebook in Film Making*, edited by Alan Rosenthal, 401–15. Berkeley: University of California Press.

Borum Chattoo, Caty. 2020. *Story Movements: How Documentaries Empower People and Inspire Social Change*. New York: Oxford University Press.

Borum Chattoo, Caty, Varsha Ramani, and Danage Norwood. 2020. "*Milwaukee 53206*" *Impact Report*. Center for Media and Social Impact, School of Communication, American University, Washington, DC. https://cmsimpact.org/wp-content/uploads/2016/08/CMSI_Milwaukee_Report.pdf.

Bourdieu, Pierre. 1993. *The Field of Cultural Production: Essays on Art and Literature*. New York: Columbia University Press.

Boynton, Robert S. 2004. "How to Make a Guerrilla Documentary." *New York Times Magazine*, July 11, 2004, 20–23.

Brave New Films. 2016. *Mass Incarceration: A Study on Building Capacity for Institutional Change in America's Unjust Prison System*. Report.

Brave New Foundation. 2012. *Rethink Afghanistan: Study of Effectiveness and Messaging Success, 2009–2012*. Report.

Burton, Orisanmi. 2015. "Black Lives Matter: A Critique of Anthropology." Hot Spots, *Fieldsights*, June 29, 2015. https://culanth.org/fieldsights/691-black-lives-matter-a-critique-of-anthropology.

Caldwell, John Thornton. 2008. *Production Culture: Industrial Reflexivity and Critical Practice in Film and Television*. Durham, NC: Duke University Press.

Caldwell, John Thornton. 2013. "Para-industry: Researching Hollywood's Blackwaters." *Cinema Journal* 52 (3): 157–65.

Caton, Steven. 1999. *Lawrence of Arabia: A Film's Anthropology*. Berkeley: University of California Press.

Cherstich, Igor, Martin Holbraad, and Nico Tassi. 2020. *Anthropologies of Revolution: Forging Time, People, and Worlds*. Oakland: University of California Press.

Chicago Women's Liberation Union. 1971. "How to Start Your Own Consciousness-Raising Group." Accessed January 27, 2021. http://www.cwluherstory.com/CWLUArchive/crcwlu.html.

Christensen, Christian. 2009. "Political Documentary, Online Organization and Activist Synergies." *Studies in Documentary Film* 3 (2): 77–94.

Combs, James E., and Sarah T. Combs. 1994. *Film Propaganda and American Politics: An Analysis and Filmography*. New York: Garland.

Curtis, Suz. 2015. "Personal Affect: The Impact of Measuring Impact." *Documentary* (Summer): 33–35.

De Genova, Nicholas. 2020. "'Everything Is Permitted': Trump, White Supremacy, Fascism." *Public Anthropologies* (blog), *American Anthropologist*, March 23, 2020. http://www.americananthropologist.org/2020/03/23/everything-is-permitted-trump-white-supremacy-fascism/.

Democracy Now. 2018. "Prof. Jason Stanley in Wake of Kavanaugh's Confirmation: Fascism Cannot Operate without Patriarchy." *Democracy Now*, October 12, 2018. Accessed October 13, 2018. https://www.democracynow.org/2018/10/12/prof-jason-stanley.

Dornfeld, Barry. 1998. *Producing Public Television, Producing Public Culture*. Princeton, NJ: Princeton University Press.

Downing, John D. H. 2001. *Radical Media: Rebellious Communication and Social Movements*. Thousand Oaks, CA: Sage.

Durham, Meenakshi Gigi, and Douglas M. Kellner, eds. 2006. *Media and Cultural Studies: Keywords*. Rev. ed. Malden, MA: Blackwell.

Edwards, David B. 2005. "Print Islam: Media and Religious Revolution in Afghanistan." In *Social Movements: An Anthropological Reader*, edited by June Nash, 99–116. Malden, MA: Blackwell.

Eley, Geoff. 1992. "Nations, Publics, and Political Cultures: Placing Habermas in the Nineteenth Century." In *Habermas and the Public Sphere*, edited by Craig Calhoun, 289–339. Cambridge, MA: MIT Press.

Escobar, Arturo. 1992. "Culture, Practice and Politics: Anthropology and the Study of Social Movements." *Critique of Anthropology* 12 (4): 394–432.

Espinosa, Julio García. 1979. "For an Imperfect Cinema." Translated by J. Burton. *Jump Cut: A Review of Contemporary Media*, no. 20 (May): 24–26.

Fallon, Kris. 2019. *Where Truth Lies: Digital Culture and Documentary Media after 9/11*. Oakland: University of California Press.

Fields, Alison Byrne. 2014. "Films Are Films: Measuring the Social Impact of Documentary Films." *Philanthropy News Digest*, July 23, 2014. https://pndblog.typepad.com/pndblog/2014/07/films-are-films-measuring-the-social-impact-of-documentary-films.html.

Finke, Nikki. 2006. "Senate Dems Probe Iraq Profiteering per Robert Greenwald's New 'Iraq for Sale.'" *Deadline*, September 18, 2006. https://deadline.com/2006/09/senate-dems-probe-iraq-profiteering-charges-made-in-robert-greenwalds-new-iraq-for-sale-dvd-583/.

Fish, Adam. 2013. "Participatory Television: Convergence, Crowdsourcing, and Neoliberalism." *Communication, Culture and Critique* 6 (3): 372–95.

Forman, James, Jr. 2017. *Locking Up Our Own: Crime and Punishment in Black America*. New York: Farrar, Straus and Giroux.

Foucault, Michel. (1977) 1980. "Truth and Power." In *Power/Knowledge: Selected Interviews and Other Writings, 1972–1977*, edited by Colin Gordon, 109–33. New York: Pantheon Books.

Fox, Richard G., and Orin Starn, eds. 1997. *Between Resistance and Revolution: Cultural Politics and Social Protest*. New Brunswick, NJ: Rutgers University Press.

Fraser, Nancy. 1992. "Rethinking the Public Sphere: A Contribution to the Critique of Actually Existing Democracy." In *Habermas and the Public Sphere*, edited by Craig Calhoun, 109–42. Cambridge, MA: MIT Press.

Fraser, Nick. 2019. *Say What Happened: A Story of Documentaries*. London: Faber and Faber.

Freire, Paulo. (1970) 2000. *Pedagogy of the Oppressed*. Translated by M. B. Ramos. New York: Bloomsbury Academic.

Freire, Paulo. 2004. *Pedagogy of Indignation*. Boulder, CO: Paradigm.

Gabriel, Teshome H. 1985. "Xala: A Cinema of Wax and Gold." In *Jumpcut: Hollywood Politics and Counter-cinema*, edited by Peter Steven, 334–43. Toronto: Between the Lines.

Gaines, Jane M. 1999. "Political Mimesis." In *Collecting Visible Evidence*, edited by Jane M. Gaines and Michael Renov, 84–102. Minneapolis: University of Minnesota Press.

Gaines, Jane M. 2007. "The Production of Outrage: The Iraq War and the Radical Documentary Tradition." *Framework: The Journal of Cinema and Media* 48 (2): 36–55.

Gaines, Jane M. 2015. "Second Thoughts on 'The Production of Outrage: The Iraq War and the Radical Documentary Tradition.'" In *A Companion to Contemporary Documentary Film*, edited by Alexandra Juhasz and Alisa Lebow, 410–30. Malden, MA: Wiley-Blackwell.

Gaines, Jane M., and Michael Renov, eds. 1999. *Collecting Visible Evidence*. Minneapolis: University of Minnesota Press.

Ganti, Tejaswini. 2012. *Producing Bollywood: Inside the Contemporary Hindi Film Industry*. Durham, NC: Duke University Press.

Garza, Alicia. 2014. "A Herstory of the #BlackLivesMatter Movement." *Feminist Wire*, October 7, 2014. http://www.thefeministwire.com/2014/10/blacklivesmatter-2.

Gibb, Robert. 2001. "Toward an Anthropology of Social Movements." *Journal des Anthropologues*, nos. 85–86, 233–53. https://doi.org/10.4000/jda.2904.

Ginsburg, Faye D. 1993. "Aboriginal Media and the Australian Imaginary." *Public Culture* 5 (3): 557–78.

Ginsburg, Faye D. 1997. "'From Little Things, Big Things Grow': Indigenous Media and Cultural Activism." In *Between Resistance and Revolution: Cultural Politics and Social Protest*, edited by Richard G. Fox and Orin Starn, 118–44. London: Routledge.

Ginsburg, Faye D. 1999. "Shooting Back: From Ethnographic Film to the Anthropology of Media." In *A Companion to Film Theory*, edited by Toby Miller and Robert Stam, 295–322. London: Blackwell.

Ginsburg, Faye D. 2002. "Screen Memories: Resignifying the Traditional in Indigenous Media." In *Media Worlds: Anthropology on New Terrain*, edited by Faye D. Ginsburg, Lila Abu-Lughod, and Brian Larkin, 39–57. Berkeley: University of California Press.

Ginsburg, Faye D., Lila Abu-Lughod, and Brian Larkin, eds. 2002. *Media Worlds: Anthropology on New Terrain*. Berkeley: University of California Press.

Gitlin, Todd. 1980. *The Whole World Is Watching: Mass Media in the Making and Unmaking of the New Left*. Berkeley: University of California Press.

Goodwin, Jeff, and James M. Jasper, eds. 2015. *The Social Movements Reader: Cases and Concepts*, 3rd ed. Malden, MA: Wiley-Blackwell.

Goodwin, Jeff, James M. Jasper, and Francesca Polletta, eds. 2001. *Passionate Politics: Emotions and Social Movements*. Chicago: University of Chicago Press.

Gordon, Deborah A. 1995. "Conclusion: Culture Writing Women: Inscribing Feminist Anthropology." In *Women Writing Culture*, edited by Ruth

Behar and Deborah A. Gordon, 429–41. Berkeley: University of California Press.

Gould, Deborah B. 2015. "The Emotion Work of Movements." In *The Social Movements Reader*, edited by Jeff Goodwin and James M. Jasper, 254–65. Malden, MA: Wiley-Blackwell.

Graeber, David. 2002. "The New Anarchists." *New Left Review*, no. 13 (January–February): 61–73.

Graeber, David. 2009. *Direct Action: An Ethnography*. Oakland, CA: AK Press.

Gramlich, John. 2021. "America's Incarceration Rate Falls to Lowest Level since 1995." *Pew Research Center*, August 16, 2021. https://www.pewresearch.org/fact-tank/2021/08/16.

Gramsci, Antonio. 1971. *Selections from Prison Notebooks*. Edited and translated by Quintin Hoare and Geoffrey Nowell Smith. New York: International Publishers.

Gregg, Melissa, and Gregory J. Seigworth, eds. 2010. *The Affect Theory Reader*. Durham, NC: Duke University Press.

Gregory, Steven. 2007. "Structures of the Imagination." In *The Devil behind the Mirror: Globalization and Politics in the Dominican Republic*, 92–129. Berkeley: University of California Press.

Griffin, Roger, ed. 1995. "General Introduction." In *Fascism*, 1–12. Oxford: Oxford University Press.

Gross, Larry, John Stuart Katz, and Jay Ruby, eds. 1988. *Image Ethics: The Moral Rights of Subjects in Photographs, Film, and Television*. New York: Oxford University Press.

Grossberg, Lawrence, Cary Nelson, and Paula A. Treichler, eds. 1992. *Cultural Studies*. New York: Routledge.

Gutiérrez, Gustavo. 1973. *A Theology of Liberation*. Maryknoll, NY: Orbis Books.

Habermas, Jürgen. (1962) 1991. *The Structural Transformation of the Public Sphere: An Inquiry into a Category of Bourgeois Society*. Translated by Thomas Burger. Cambridge, MA: MIT Press.

Hale, Charles R., ed. 2008. *Engaging Contradictions: Theory, Politics, and Methods of Activist Scholarship*. Berkeley: University of California Press.

Hall, Stuart. 1992. "Cultural Studies and Its Theoretical Legacies." In *Cultural Studies*, edited by Lawrence Grossberg, Cary Nelson, and Paula Treichler, 277–94. New York: Routledge.

Hall, Stuart, Dorothy Hobson, Andrew Lowe, and Paul Willis, eds. 1980. *Culture, Media, Language*. London: Hutchinson.

Hamm, Theodore. 2008. *The New Blue Media: How Michael Moore, MoveOn.org, Jon Stewart and Company Are Transforming Progressive Politics*. New York: New Press.

Hardt, Michael. 1999. "Affective Labor." *boundary* 26 (2): 89–100.

Haynes, John. 2007. "Documentary as Social Justice Activism: The Textual and Political Strategies of Robert Greenwald and Brave New Films." *49th Parallel* 21 (Autumn): 1–16.

Haynes, John, and Jo Littler. 2007. "Documentary as Political Activism: An Interview with Robert Greenwald." *Cinéaste* 32 (4): 26–29.

Herman, Edward, and Noam Chomsky. 1988. *Manufacturing Consent: The Political Economy of the Mass Media*. New York: Pantheon.

Herndon, Astead W. 2020. "For Black Women, a Long Fight to Change How Georgia Voted." *New York Times*, December 4, 2020.

Hill, Christopher. 1972. *The World Turned Upside Down: Radical Ideas during the English Revolution*. London: Penguin Books.

Hill, Christopher. 1993. "A Note on Liberation Theology." In *The English Bible and the Seventeenth-Century Revolution*, 447–52. London: Penguin.

Ho, Karen, and Jillian Cavanaugh. 2019. Introduction to "What Happened to Social Facts?" Vital Topics Forum (special section), *American Anthropologist* 121 (1): 160–204.

Horkheimer, Max, and Theodor W. Adorno. (1944) 2006. "The Culture Industry: Enlightenment as Mass Deception." Translated by E. Jephcott. In *Media and Cultural Studies: Keyworks*, edited by Meenakshi Gigi Durham and Douglas M. Kellner, 41–72. Malden, MA: Blackwell.

Hughes, Stephen Putnam. 2011. "Anthropology and the Problem of Audience Reception." In *Made to Be Seen: Perspectives on the History of Visual Anthropology*, edited by Marcus Banks and Jay Ruby, 288–312. Chicago: University of Chicago Press.

Johnson, Arne. 2007. ". . . and Nothing but the Truth?" *Filmmaker* (Fall): 90–91, 106–7.

Jones, Amelia, ed. 2010. *The Feminism and Visual Culture Reader*. London: Routledge.

Juris, Jeffrey S. 2008. *Networking Futures: The Movements against Corporate Globalization*. Durham, NC: Duke University Press.

Juris, Jeffrey S., and Alex Khasnabish, eds. 2013. *Insurgent Encounters: Transnational Activism, Ethnography, and the Political*. Durham, NC: Duke University Press.

Kaplan, E. Ann. 1984. "Theory and Practice of the Realist Documentary Form in Harlan County, U.S.A." In *"Show Us Life": Toward a History and Aesthetics of the Committed Documentary*, edited by Thomas Waugh, 212–22. Metuchen, NJ: Scarecrow.

Kellner, Douglas. 2010. *Cinema Wars: Hollywood Film and Politics in the Bush-Cheney Era*. Malden, MA: Wiley-Blackwell.

Koch Brothers Exposed: A Brave New Foundation Campaign. n.d. Impact Report. Culver City, CA: Brave New Foundation.

Kurik, Bob. 2016. "Emerging Subjectivity in Protest." In *The Sage Handbook of Resistance*, edited by David Courpasson and Steven Vallas, 51–77. Thousand Oaks, CA: Sage.

Larkin, Brian. 2008. *Signal and Noise: Media, Infrastructure, and Urban Culture in Nigeria.* Durham, NC: Duke University Press.

Lazere, Donald. 1987. *American Media and Mass Culture: Left Perspectives.* Berkeley: University of California Press.

Lopez, Lori Kido, ed. 2020. *Race and Media: Critical Approaches.* New York: NYU Press.

Low, Setha M., and Sally Engle Merry. 2010. "Engaged Anthropology: Diversity and Dilemmas." *Current Anthropology* 51 (S2): 201–26.

MacDonald, Scott. 2013. *American Ethnographic Film and Personal Documentary: The Cambridge Turn.* Berkeley: University of California Press.

Mackey-Kallis, Susan. 2008. "Talking Heads Rock the House: Robert Greenwald's *Uncovered: The War on Iraq.*" In *The Rhetoric of the New Political Documentary*, edited by Thomas W. Benson and Brian J. Snee, 153–72. Carbondale: Southern Illinois University Press.

MacLean, Nancy. 2017. *Democracy in Chains: A Deep History of the Radical Right's Stealth Plan for America.* New York: Penguin Books.

Mahon, Maureen. 2000. "The Visible Evidence of Cultural Producers." *Annual Reviews in Anthropology* 29:467–92.

Mankekar, Purnima. 1999. *Screening Culture, Viewing Politics: An Ethnography of Television, Womanhood, and Nation in Postcolonial India.* Durham, NC: Duke University Press.

Mankekar, Purnima. 2015. *Unsettling India: Affect, Temporality, Transnationality.* Durham, NC: Duke University Press.

Marcus, Daniel. 2016. "Documentary and Video Activism." In *Contemporary Documentary*, edited by Daniel Marcus and Selmin Kara, 187–203. London: Routledge.

Martin, Sylvia J. 2017. *Haunted: An Ethnography of the Hollywood and Hong Kong Media Industries.* Oxford: Oxford University Press.

Mayer, Jane. 2016. *Dark Money: The Hidden History of the Billionaires behind the Rise of the Radical Right.* New York: Anchor Books.

Mayer, Vicki, Miranda J. Banks, and John Thornton Caldwell, eds. 2009. *Production Studies: Cultural Studies of Media Industries.* New York: Routledge.

Mazzarella, William. 2010. "Affect: What Is It Good For?" In *Enchantments of Modernity: Empire, Nation, Globalization*, edited by Saurabh Dube, 291–309. London: Routledge.

McEnteer, James. 2006. *Shooting the Truth: The Rise of American Political Documentaries*. Westport, CT: Praeger.

Meyer, David S. 2015. "How Social Movements Matter." In *The Social Movements Reader: Cases and Concepts*, 3rd ed., edited by Jeff Goodwin and James M. Jasper, 386–90. Malden, MA: Wiley-Blackwell.

Miller, Toby. 1998. "The Truth Is a Murky Path: Technologies of Citizenship and the Visual." In *Technologies of Truth*, 182–215. Minneapolis: University of Minnesota Press.

Musser, Charles. 2007. "War, Documentary and Iraq Dossier: Film Truth in the Age of George W. Bush." *Framework* 48 (2): 9–35.

Nash, June, ed. 2005. *Social Movements: An Anthropological Reader*. Malden, MA: Blackwell.

Neiwert, David. 2017. *Alt-America: The Rise of the Radical Right in the Age of Trump*. London: Verso.

Nichols, Bill. (1972) 2016. "San Francisco Newsreel: Collectives, Politics, Films." In *Speaking Truths with Film: Evidence, Ethics, Politics in Documentary*, 201–19. Oakland: University of California Press.

Nichols, Bill. 1978. "*38 Families, Redevelopment. Revolution until Victory: The Beginning of Our Victory*. New from California Newsreel." *Jump Cut: A Review of Contemporary Media*, no. 17 (April): 10–13.

Nichols, Bill. 1981. *Ideology and the Image: Social Representation in the Cinema and Other Media*. Bloomington: Indiana University Press.

Nichols, Bill. 1991. *Representing Reality: Issues and Concepts in Documentary*. Bloomington: Indiana University Press.

Nichols, Bill. 2005. "The Voice of Documentary." In *New Challenges for Documentary*, 2nd ed., edited by Alan Rosenthal and John Corner, 17–33. Manchester: Manchester University Press.

Nichols, Bill. 2016a. "The Political Documentary and the Question of Impact." In *Speaking Truths with Film: Evidence, Ethics, Politics in Documentary*, 220–29. Oakland: University of California Press.

Nichols, Bill. 2016b. *Speaking Truths with Film: Evidence, Ethics, Politics in Documentary*. Oakland: University of California Press.

Nussbaum, Martha C. 2016. *Anger and Forgiveness: Resentment, Generosity, Justice*. New York: Oxford University Press.

Ohmann, Richard, ed. 1996. *Making and Selling Culture*. Hanover, NH: Wesleyan University Press / University Press of New England.

Ortner, Sherry B. 1995. "Resistance and the Problem of Ethnographic Refusal." *Comparative Studies in Society and History* 37 (1): 173–93.

Ortner, Sherry B. 1999. *Life and Death on Mt. Everest: Sherpas and Himalayan Mountaineering*. Princeton, NJ: Princeton University Press.

Ortner, Sherry B. 2006. "Power and Projects: Reflections on Agency." In *Anthropology and Social Theory: Culture, Power, and the Acting Subject*, 129–54. Durham, NC: Duke University Press.

Ortner, Sherry B. 2010. "Access: Reflections on Studying Up in Hollywood." *Ethnography* 11 (2): 211–33.

Ortner, Sherry B. 2012. "Against Hollywood: American Independent Film as a Critical Cultural Movement." HAU: *Journal of Ethnographic Theory* 2 (2): 1–21. https://www.haujournal.org/index.php/hau/article/view/hau2.2 .002/297.

Ortner, Sherry B. 2013a. "Not a History Lesson: The Erasure of Politics in American Cinema." *Visual Anthropology Review* 29 (2): 77–88.

Ortner, Sherry B. 2013b. *Not Hollywood: Independent Film at the Twilight of the American Dream.* Durham, NC: Duke University Press.

Ortner, Sherry B. 2014. "Too Soon for Post-feminism: The Ongoing Life of Patriarchy in Neoliberal America." *History and Anthropology* 25 (4): 530–49.

Ortner, Sherry B. 2016. "Dark Anthropology and Its Others: Theory since the Eighties." HAU: *Journal of Ethnographic Theory* 6 (1): 47–73. https://www .haujournal.org/index.php/hau/issue/view/hau6.1.

Ortner, Sherry B. 2017. "Social Impact without Social Justice: Film and Politics in the Neoliberal Landscape." *American Ethnologist* 44 (3): 528–39.

Ortner, Sherry B. 2019. "Practicing Engaged Anthropology." *Anthropology of This Century*, no. 25 (May). http://aotcpress.com.

Ortner, Sherry B. 2020. "Racializing Patriarchy: Lessons from Police Brutality." In *Gender, Considered: Feminist Reflections across the US Social Sciences*, edited by Sarah Fenstermaker and Abigail J. Stewart, 137–64. Cham, Switzerland: Palgrave Macmillan.

Orwell, George. 1949. *1984.* New York: New American Library.

Partis, Michael. 2019. "The Making of Racial Caste in Post-truth America." *American Anthropologist* 121 (1): 170–71.

Paxton, Robert. 2005. "What Is Fascism?" In *The Anatomy of Fascism*, 206–20. London: Penguin Random House.

Press, Andrea L. 1991. *Women Watching Television: Gender, Class, and Generation in the American Television Experience.* Philadelphia: University of Pennsylvania Press.

Press, Andrea L., and Francesca Tripodi. 2021. *Media-Ready Feminism and Everyday Sexism: How U.S. Audiences Create Meaning across Platforms.* Albany: SUNY Press.

Rabinowitz, Paula. 1994. *They Must Be Represented: The Politics of Documentary.* New York: Verso.

Ralph, Laurence. 2017. "Alibi: The Extralegal Force Embedded in the Law (United States)." In *Writing the World of Policing: The Difference Ethnog-*

raphy Makes, edited by Didier Fassin, 248–68. Chicago: University of Chicago Press.

Ralph, Laurence, and Kerry Chance. 2014. "Legacies of Fear: From Rodney King's Beating to Trayvon Martin's Death." *Transition*, no. 113, 137–43.

Redstockings. 1969. *Manifesto*. Accessed January 27, 2021. https://www .redstockings.org/index.php/rs-manifesto.

Renov, Michael. 2004. "Early Newsreel: The Construction of a Political Imaginary for the New Left." In *The Subject of Documentary*, 3–20. Minneapolis: University of Minnesota Press.

Rethink Afghanistan: Brave New Foundation Study of Effectiveness and Messaging Success. n.d. [2012]. Culver City, CA: Brave New Foundation.

Rosenfeld, Sophia. 2019. *Democracy and Truth: A Short History*. Philadelphia: University of Pennsylvania Press.

Rosenthal, Alan. 1980. *The Documentary Conscience: A Casebook in Filmmaking*. Berkeley: University of California Press.

Rouch, Jean. 2003. *Ciné-ethnography*. Edited and translated by Steven Feld. Minneapolis: University of Minnesota Press.

Rouse, Carolyn Moxley, John L. Jackson Jr., and Marla F. Frederick, eds. 2016. *Televised Redemption: Black Religious Media and Racial Empowerment*. New York: NYU Press.

Roussel, Violaine, and Bleuwenn Lechaux. 2010. *Voicing Dissent: American Artists and the War on Iraq*. London: Routledge.

Rutherford, Danilyn. 2016. "Affect Theory and the Empirical." *Annual Review of Anthropology* 45:285–300.

Schiller, Naomi. 2018. *Channeling the State: Community Media and Popular Politics in Venezuela*. Durham, NC: Duke University Press.

Scott, James. 1985. *Weapons of the Weak: Everyday Forms of Peasant Resistance*. New Haven, CT: Yale University Press.

Sewell, William H., Jr. 2005. "Historical Events as Transformations of Structures: Inventing Revolution at the Bastille." In *Logics of History: Social Theory and Social Transformation*, 225–70. Chicago: University of Chicago Press.

Shah, Alpa. 2019. *Nightmarch: Among India's Revolutionary Guerrillas*. Chicago: University of Chicago Press.

Shohat, Ella, and Robert Stam. 1994. *Unthinking Eurocentrism: Multiculturalism and the Media*. London: Routledge.

Smithline, Lisa. 2005. "Telling Stories, Building Movements: Can a Film Change Wal-Mart?" *Social Policy* (Fall): 6–8.

Solanas, Fernando, and Octavio Getino. 1976. "Towards a Third Cinema." In *Movies and Methods: An Anthology*, vol. 1, edited by Bill Nichols, 44–64. Tucson: University of Arizona Press.

Solomon, Akiba, and Kenrya Rankin. 2019. *How We Fight White Supremacy: A Field Guide to Black Resistance*. New York: Bold Type Books.

Spence, Louise, and Vinicius Navarro. 2011. *Crafting Truth: Documentary Form and Meaning*. New Brunswick, NJ: Rutgers University Press.

Sperling, Nicole. 2020. "Khashoggi as Subject Is Hard Sell." *New York Times*, December 26, 2020.

Stanley, Jason. 2018. *How Fascism Works: The Politics of Us and Them*. New York: Random House.

Steven, Peter, ed. 1985. *Jump Cut: Hollywood, Politics, and Counter-cinema*. Toronto: Between the Lines.

Stringer, Tish. 2013. "This Is What Democracy Looked Like." In *Insurgent Encounters: Transnational Activism, Ethnography, and the Political*, edited by Jeffrey S. Juris and Alex Khasnabish, 318–41. Durham, NC: Duke University Press.

Tarrow, Sidney G. 2011. *Power in Movement: Social Movements and Contentious Politics*. Rev. and updated 3rd ed. Cambridge: Cambridge University Press.

Taylor, Keeanga-Yamahtta. 2017. *How We Get Free: Black Feminism and the Combahee River Collective*. Chicago: Haymarket Books.

Terrill, Robert E. 2008. "Mimesis and Miscarriage in *Unprecedented*." In *The Rhetoric of the New Political Documentary*, edited by Thomas W. Benson and Brian J. Snee, 131–52. Carbondale: Southern Illinois University Press.

Theodossopoulos, Dimitrios, ed. 2017. *De-pathologizing Resistance: Anthropological Interventions*. London: Routledge.

Thompson, E. P. 1963. *The Making of the English Working Class*. London: Victor Golancz.

Traube, Elizabeth G. 1992. *Dreaming Identities: Class, Gender, and Generation in 1980s Hollywood Movies*. Boulder, CO: Westview.

Turner, Terence. 2002. "Representation, Politics, and Cultural Imagination in Indigenous Video: General Points and Kayapo Examples." In *Media Worlds*, edited by Faye D. Ginsburg, Lila Abu-Lughod, and Brian Larkin, 75–89. Berkeley: University of California Press.

Vargas, Joao. 2015. "Black Lives Don't Matter." Hot Spots, *Fieldsights*, June 29, 2015. https://cultanth.org/fieldsights/695-black-lives-dont-matter.

Vasi, Ion Bogdan, Edward T. Walker, John J. Johnson, and Hui Fen Tan. 2015. "'No Fracking Way!': Documentary Film, Discursive Opportunity, and Local Opposition against Hydraulic Fracturing in the United States, 2010 to 2013." *American Sociological Review* 80 (5): 934–59.

Vásquez, Manuel A. 1998. *The Brazilian Popular Church and the Crisis of Modernity*. Cambridge: Cambridge University Press.

Walsh, Joan. 2021. "Georgia Goes Blue." *The Nation*, February 8/15, 2021, 6.

Waugh, Thomas, ed. 1984. *"Show Us Life": Toward a History and Aesthetics of the Committed Documentary*. Metuchen, NJ: Scarecrow.

Whiteman, David. 2004. "Out of the Theaters and into the Streets: A Coalition Model of the Political Impact of Documentary Film and Video." *Political Communication* 21 (1): 51–69.

Williams, Bianca C. 2015. "#BlackLivesMatter: Anti-Black Racism, Police Violence, and Resistance." Hot Spots, *Fieldsights*, June 29, 2015. https://culanth.org/fieldsights/696-blacklivesmatter-anti-black-racism-police-violence-and-resistance.

Williams, Linda. 1998. "Mirrors without Memories: Truth, History, and *The Thin Blue Line*." In *Documenting the Documentary: Close Readings of Documentary Film and Video*, edited by Barry Keith Grant and Jeannette Sloniowki, 379–96. Detroit: Wayne State University Press.

Williams, Raymond. 1977. *Marxism and Literature*. Oxford: Oxford University Press.

Winston, Brian. 1995. *Claiming the Real: The Documentary Film Revisited*. London: BFI Publications.

Index